Swords and Plowshares

For permission to reprint, please contact:

URJ Press
633 Third Avenue
New York, NY 10017–6778

(212) 650–4124
press@urj.org

Library of Congress Cataloging-in-Publication Data

Goldberg, Edwin C.
    Swords and plowshares : Jewish views of war and peace / Edwin C. Goldberg
        p. cm.
    ISBN 0-8074-0943-X (alk. paper)
    1. War–Religious aspects–Judaism. 2. Rabbinical literature. 3. Rabbinical
literature–History and criticism. 4. War–Biblical teaching. 5. War in rabbinical
literature. 6. United States–History, Military–20th century. 7. Israel–History,
Military. I. Title.

    BM538.P3G65 2006
    296.3'827–dc22

                                                                2006040373

Designer: Shaul Akri
Typesetting: El Ot Ltd., Tel Aviv
This book is printed on acid-free paper
Text copyright © 2006 by Edwin Goldberg
Manufactured in the United States of America
10 9 8 7 6 5 4 3 2 1

Swords and Plowshares

Jewish Views of War and Peace

Edwin C. Goldberg

URJ PRESS
FOR A LIFETIME OF JEWISH LEARNING

New York, New York

Contents

Preface   vii

Acknowledgments   viii

Permissions   ix

Background: Reasons for War   xi

1. Why Do We Fight? Violence and the Human Condition   1

2. *Milchemet Chovah*: Required Wars   12

3. *Milchemet R'shut*: Optional Wars   22

4. *Milchemet Mitzvah*: Defensive Wars   35

5. Launching a Preemptive War   45

6. Exhortation to Fight   52

7. Military Exemptions   59

8. The Treatment of Prisoners of War   71

9. The Treatment of Natural Resources during War   85

10. Making Peace   95

Conclusion   105

Glossary of Terms and Sources   109

Preface

The subject of war and peace has been all too relevant during the last several years. The second intifada, the terrorist attacks of 9/11, and the wars in Afghanistan and Iraq have constantly been in the headlines and on our minds. Therefore it has also been an appropriate time to ponder the perspective of the Jewish tradition regarding issues of war and peace.

In its simple wisdom, the Book of Ecclesiastes declares that there is a time for war and a time for peace, *eit milchamah v'eit shalom*. What is far more complex is determining *when* there should be peace and when there should be war, and how such wars should be fought. There are no easy answers to such questions, but throughout its history traditional Jewish sources—beginning with the Bible—have offered a variety of insights into when to wage war, how to wage war, and per-haps most importantly, when to work for peace.

The great textual sources of Judaism, such as the Bible, the Talmud, the midrash, and later codes and com-mentaries, are not monolithic when it comes to questions of war and peace, but careful study of these texts offers an awareness of a general approach toward this most human and challenging subject. The student of Jewish texts in this area will see that, as history unfolds, Jewish leaders transformed them-selves from what we might call proponents of "holy war" to advocates of peace in most—although not all—circumstances.

While the material in this book is presented topically and not chronologically, this trend will be noticeable.

This book is not an exhaustive study of the Jewish views of war and peace. It is meant to be a compendium of various Jewish texts that deal with the subject. Each text is presented in Hebrew and English, followed by study questions and commentary to help the reader explore the intricacies of the texts. It is hoped that through such guided study, the reader will appreciate the nuances and basic characteristics of the texts, as well as their messages concerning war and peace. Each chapter concludes with more general questions regarding the ethical implications of the topic and additional texts related to the topic. A glossary of terms and sources is provided at the end of the book.

Acknowledgments

I want to thank Rabbi Hara Person of the URJ Press, who has carefully edited this volume. I know that she was helped by Victor Ney, Michael Goldberg, Debra Hirsch Corman, Ron Ghatan, Lauren Dubin, and Dahlia Schoenberg. I would also like to thank those from the Commission on Social Action and Religious Action Center who provided help, in particular Rabbi Marla Feldman and Rabbi David Saperstein.

I am grateful for the following previously published works whose insights have been helpful in the preparation of this book:

Artson, Bradley Shavit. *A Jewish Response to War and Nuclear Annihilation*. New York: United Synagogue Commission on Jewish Education, 1988.

Gendler, Everett E. "War and the Jewish Tradition" in *Contemporary Jewish Ethics*, edited by Menachem Mark Kellner, pp. 189–210. New York: Hebrew Publishing Co., 1978.

Homolka, Walter, and Albert H. Friedlander. *The Gate to Perfection: The Idea of Peace in Jewish Thought*. Providence: Berghahn, 1994.

Washofsky, Mark. "Preventive War." CCAR Responsa 5762.8.

Finally, I wish to thank Temple Judea, in Coral Gables, Florida, for the granting of the time needed to complete this book.

Permissions

Background:
Reasons for War

Throughout the book, various wars fought by the United States and by Israel will be mentioned. In order to help the reader place such references in context what follows is a basic list of the central wars fought by the U.S. and Israel. When explaining the Jewish views toward war, it is important to consider the reasons for different wars. However, keep in mind that these explanations are highly abbreviated.

General History

World War I. The chief reason for this war was the tension among various European states, especially Germany, Italy, France, and England. The war began after the assassination of Archduke Franz Ferdinand, heir to the Austro-Hungarian throne, on June 28, 1914, in Sarajevo. He was killed by a Serbian nationalist secret society. This death set in motion a chain reaction that eventually led to the outbreak of war. First, the Austro-Hungarian Empire decided it needed to retaliate against Serbia, which it (probably falsely) concluded had a hand in the assassination. Its demand that the Serbians hand over the guilty party was seen by Serbia as a challenge to its sovereignty. This dispute between Serbia and the Austro-Hungarian Empire drew the attention of Russia, France, and England (on the side of Serbia) and Germany (on the side of the Austro-Hungarian Empire) and in a classic example of "one thing led to another" brought about a world war. A significant reason for the participation of these countries was the treaties that had been signed promising support in the event of war.

World War II. Compared to World War I, the reasons for this war are relatively more clear and well-known. In Europe, the Nazis rose to power because of the humiliation of the peace settlement following World War I. The economic collapse of Germany following the peace settlement helped prepare the country for its embrace of Hitler and his genocidal war against the Jews. In turn, Hitler's aggression against Europe eventually led to the inevitable war. In Asia, the aggression of the Japanese against China led to an American embargo against Japan. Japan, desperate for oil, attempted to delay America from entering the war with an attack on its fleet at Pearl Harbor. Although the attack successfully made it difficult for America to immediately respond to Japan with military action, America declared war on Japan the following day. Germany then declared war on the United States, in part because of the treaty that Germany had with Japan.

Korean War. Although the war (officially in the United States called a "police action") lasted only from 1950 to 1953, it reflected (and still reflects) a much longer period of tension between China to the north and the democratic countries of the West. The actual war was between the Republic of Korea (i.e., South Korea) and the Democratic People's Republic of Korea (i.e., North Korea). As in World War I, this "small war" became the battleground of the great powers, leading to the involvement of the United States and the United Nations on one side, and the People's Republic of China on the other (with the Soviet Union—another Communist country—interested as well). In general, the war became an issue of containing or spreading Communism. After three years of fighting, there was no change in the status quo.

Vietnam War. Like the Korean War, the issues that led to war were complex. The American involvement in the war followed the failed attempt of the French to recolonize Vietnam in the 1950s. As in Korea, the American effort stemmed from the desire to keep Communism in check. Some events that led to the war were the declaration of independence of Vietnam in 1945, leading to the division of the country into two, North Vietnam and South Vietnam. The Communist forces in North Vietnam attempted to throw off French colonial rule, leading to war with the French. The French left in defeat, and the division between the two countries was recognized by the Geneva Conference on Indochina in 1954. The United States declared its support for the South Vietnam government. War soon broke out between North Vietnam and South Vietnam. In the 1960s, American troops began to arrive. In 1964, North

Vietnam was accused of attacking a U.S. destroyer in the Gulf of Tonkin, leading the U.S. Congress to give President Lyndon Johnson permission to use force to fight North Vietnam, thus escalating the war and America's involvement.

Gulf War (I and II). The first Gulf War, called Desert Storm, began in August of 1990, when Saddam Hussein, the dictator of Iraq, invaded Kuwait, an oil-rich Arab nation on friendly terms with the United States. After warning Hussein to retreat, the United States led an international coalition of forces against Iraq, with the goal of freeing Kuwait. After a lengthy buildup of forces, the coalition quickly subdued the Iraqis and pushed them out of Kuwait. President George H. W. Bush decided not to invade Baghdad, and thus Saddam Hussein remained in power until the second Gulf War of 2003, initiated during the presidency of George W. Bush.

Israeli History

War of Independence. In May of 1948, Israel declared itself a state. Immediately, surrounding Arab armies attacked, hoping to crush the new state. Actually, the war had unofficially begun the previous November when the United Nations voted to allow the existence of a Jewish state. Arab armies that attacked included those of Egypt, Syria, Iraq, and Jordan. In the course of the war, which lasted until the middle of 1949, many Arab inhabitants of the land fled from their homes. They were kept in refugee camps on the borders of the Arab nations surrounding Israel and were not allowed to settle in the various Arab lands. At the end of hostilities, Jerusalem was declared a divided city, with the western section held in Israeli hands and the eastern portion, including the holy Old City, held by Jordan.

Sinai Campaign. In 1956, Egypt, which had never stopped being at war with Israel, despite its signing of an armistice with it in 1949, took aggressive action against Israel by closing the Straits of Tiran, a precious waterway vital to its economic survival. Israel responded by secretly planning an invasion of Egypt's Sinai Peninsula, in partnership with France and England. The campaign resulted in a victory for Israel, which captured the Sinai. However, pressure from the United States forced Israel to return the land to Egypt.

Six-Day War. In May of 1967, Egypt and Syria were declaring their intention to destroy Israel. Israel decided in early June to preemptively attack these two nations in order to destroy their war-making capability. This decision came after a very tense few weeks in which Israel feared for its very survival as a country. After the attack began, and Israel quickly won control over Egyptian and Syrian airspace, Israel sent word to Jordan, its quiet neighbor to the east, to stay out of the conflict. Nevertheless, falsely believing that the Egyptians and Syrians were winning the war, Jordanian forces attacked Jerusalem. Israel responded by sending in paratroopers, who took the Old City of Jerusalem. The other area controlled by Jordan, usually called the West Bank, was also seized by Israel, as well as the Golan Heights (which had belonged to Syria) and the Sinai Peninsula (which had belonged to Egypt) and the adjoining Gaza Strip.

Yom Kippur War. In October of 1973, Egypt and Syria, seeking to reverse its humiliating defeat in June of 1967, launched a surprise attack against Israel on Yom Kippur. Although initially slow in responding, as the war went on (for several weeks), Israel launched successful counterattacks against both Egypt and Syria.

Lebanon War. Also called Operation Peace in the Galilee, this war began in the summer of 1982. Palestinian terrorists, having been expelled from Jordan, had been using Lebanon (Israel's neighbor to the north) to launch attacks against the northern area of Israel, the Galilee. Israel invaded southern Lebanon in order to stop these attacks and then decided to continue its invasion into the Lebanese capital of Beirut.

Intifadas I and II. In 1987, the first intifada (Arabic for "uprising") began when Palestinians in the West Bank expressed their rage by throwing stones at Israeli soldiers. The uprising lasted for many years and led to the Arab-Israeli peace processes of the 1990s. In 2000, after the breakdown of the peace process, the Palestinians launched a second wave of attacks, far more violent in their use of lethal weapons.

CHAPTER ONE

Why Do We Fight?
Violence and the Human Condition

When did human violence begin? The Bible makes it clear: with the first family in history. The story of Cain and Abel is well-known. Nevertheless, most readers do not realize that the story is not merely about two brothers. It is also about one-half of the world's population. Indeed, when Cain kills Abel, he is destroying one-fourth of world humanity! The most important issue posed by this first murder is the basic question of why murder exists. Why do people kill each other? Why is there violence of any kind? Cain and Abel are not only brothers; they are paradigms for all the violent people who are to follow. In this chapter we will explore Rabbinic responses to the Cain and Abel story, found in the classic midrashic work *B'reishit Rabbah*.

Midrash is an activity in which the Rabbis of Palestine, over fifteen hundred years ago, attempted to interpret the Bible in order to understand what it says and to make it more relevant for their era. Midrash is also the name of the texts that include such interpretation. *B'reishit Rabbah* (ca. 500 C.E.) is a text of midrash that interprets the Book of Genesis. In order to appreciate the midrash, one must begin with the Torah passage upon which the midrash will comment. Our passage is the famous encounter from Genesis 4.

Text

Genesis 4:1–8

וְהָאָדָם יָדַע אֶת־חַוָּה אִשְׁתּוֹ וַתַּהַר וַתֵּלֶד אֶת־קַיִן¹
וַתֹּאמֶר קָנִיתִי אִישׁ אֶת־יְהוָה: ²וַתֹּסֶף לָלֶדֶת אֶת־אָחִיו
אֶת־הָבֶל וַיְהִי־הֶבֶל רֹעֵה צֹאן וְקַיִן הָיָה עֹבֵד אֲדָמָה:
³וַיְהִי מִקֵּץ יָמִים וַיָּבֵא קַיִן מִפְּרִי הָאֲדָמָה מִנְחָה
לַיהוָה: ⁴וְהֶבֶל הֵבִיא גַם־הוּא מִבְּכֹרוֹת צֹאנוֹ וּמֵחֶלְבֵהֶן
וַיִּשַׁע יְהוָה אֶל־הֶבֶל וְאֶל־מִנְחָתוֹ: ⁵וְאֶל־קַיִן וְאֶל־
מִנְחָתוֹ לֹא שָׁעָה וַיִּחַר לְקַיִן מְאֹד וַיִּפְּלוּ פָּנָיו: ⁶וַיֹּאמֶר
יְהוָה אֶל־קָיִן לָמָּה חָרָה לָךְ וְלָמָּה נָפְלוּ פָנֶיךָ: ⁷הֲלוֹא
אִם־תֵּיטִיב שְׂאֵת וְאִם לֹא תֵיטִיב לַפֶּתַח חַטָּאת רֹבֵץ
וְאֵלֶיךָ תְּשׁוּקָתוֹ וְאַתָּה תִּמְשָׁל־בּוֹ: ⁸וַיֹּאמֶר קַיִן אֶל־
הֶבֶל אָחִיו וַיְהִי בִּהְיוֹתָם בַּשָּׂדֶה וַיָּקָם קַיִן אֶל־הֶבֶל
אָחִיו וַיַּהַרְגֵהוּ:

2

1. The man now was intimate with his wife; she became pregnant and gave birth to Cain, saying, "Both I and the Eternal have made a man."

2. She then continued, giving birth to his brother Abel. Abel became a shepherd, while Cain tilled the soil.

3. [One day,] in the course of time, Cain brought some of his harvest as an offering to the Eternal,

4. and Abel, too, brought [an offering] from among the choice lambs of his flock and their fattest parts. The Eternal approved Abel and his offering,

5. but did not approve Cain and his offering. Cain was filled with rage; his face fell.

6. The Eternal One then said to Cain, "Why are you so angry?/Why your fallen face?/

7. Would you not do well to lift it?/For if you do not do well—/sin is a demon at the door;/you are the one it craves,/and yet you can govern it."

8. And Cain talked with Abel his brother. Then when they were in the field, Cain turned on his brother Abel and slew him.

Note that in the text God does not judge each offering the same way. God appears to favor Abel's offering because the quality of the offering was better, for as the text relates, it was "the *choice* lambs of his flock" that Abel brought. It could also be that God is favoring Abel for no specific reason, but this theory reflects an unfair behavior on the part of God and would not be consistent with the story. God appears to try to teach Cain that he need not be angry because his offering is not held in the same respect. Rather, he should learn from his mistake what to do next time.

What follows in verse 8 is the key element of the story, at least for purposes of this discussion. Cain and Abel argue, and the first act of human violence is the result. But about what did they argue? The text does not say. One modern translation (Jewish Publication Society of America, 1962) even includes an ellipsis (. . .) in the sentence, suggesting that part of the dialogue is missing from the Torah text. If we knew about what they were arguing, we could know why it is that human beings fight. This mystery is the subject of the midrashic comments that follow.

B'reishit Rabbah 22:7

"וַיֹּאמֶר קַיִן אֶל־הֶבֶל אָחִיו, וַיְהִי בִּהְיוֹתָם וְגוֹ'" — עַל מֶה הָיוּ מְדַיְּנִים? אָמְרוּ: בּוֹאוּ וּנְחַלֵּק אֶת הָעוֹלָם. אֶחָד נָטַל אֶת הַקַּרְקָעוֹת וְאֶחָד נָטַל אֶת הַמִּטַּלְטְלִין. דִּין אָמַר אַרְעָא דְאַתְּ קָאִים עֲלֵיהּ דִּידִי וְדִין אָמַר מַה דְאַתְּ לָבֵישׁ דִּידִי. דִּין אָמַר: חֲלֹץ! וְדִין אָמַר: פְּרַח! מִתּוֹךְ כָּךְ: וַיָּקָם קַיִן אֶל־הֶבֶל אָחִיו וַיַּהַרְגֵהוּ.

ר' יְהוֹשֻׁעַ מִסַּכְנִין בְּשֵׁם ר' לֵוִי אָמַר: שְׁנֵיהֶם נָטְלוּ אֶת הַקַּרְקָעוֹת וּשְׁנֵיהֶם נָטְלוּ אֶת הַמִּטַּלְטְלִים. וְעַל מֶה הָיוּ

4

מְדַיְּנִים? אֶלָּא זֶה אָמַר: בִּתְחוּמִי בֵּית הַמִּקְדָּשׁ נִבְנֶה,
וְזֶה אָמַר: בִּתְחוּמִי בֵּית הַמִּקְדָּשׁ נִבְנֶה, שֶׁנֶּאֱמַר: וַיְהִי
בִּהְיוֹתָם בַּשָּׂדֶה—וְאֵין שָׂדֶה אֶלָּא בֵּית הַמִּקְדָּשׁ, הֵיךְ
מַה דְּאַתְּ אָמַר (מיכה ג) צִיּוֹן שָׂדֶה תֵחָרֵשׁ. וּמִתּוֹךְ כָּךְ:
(בראשית ד) וַיָּקָם קַיִן אֶל־הֶבֶל אָחִיו וגו'.

יְהוּדָה בַּר אַמִּי אָמַר: עַל חַוָּה הָרִאשׁוֹנָה הָיוּ מְדַיְּנִים.
אָמַר ר' אַיְבּוּ: חַוָּה הָרִאשׁוֹנָה חָזְרָה לַעֲפָרָהּ. וְעַל מָה
הָיוּ מְדַיְּנִים? אָמַר ר' הוּנָא: תְּאוֹמָה יְתֵרָה נוֹלְדָה עִם
הֶבֶל. זֶה אָמַר: אֲנִי נוֹטְלָהּ, שֶׁאֲנִי בְּכוֹר! וְזֶה אָמַר: אֲנִי
נוֹטְלָהּ, שֶׁנּוֹלְדָה עִמִּי! וּמִתּוֹךְ כָּךְ וַיָּקָם קַיִן.

AND CAIN TALKED WITH ABEL HIS BROTHER...(Genesis 4:8).
About what did they quarrel? "Come," said they, "let us
divide the world." One took the land and the other the
movables. The former said, "The land you stand on is
mine," while the latter retorted, "What you are wearing
is mine." One said, "Strip"; the other retorted, "Fly [off
the ground]." Out of this quarrel, CAIN TURNED ON HIS
BROTHER ABEL...

Rabbi Joshua of Siknin said in Rabbi Levi's name: Both
took land and both took movables, but about what did
they quarrel? One said, "The Temple must be built in my
area," while the other claimed, "It must be built in

5

mine." For thus it is written, THEN WHEN THEY WERE IN THE FIELD: Now FIELD refers to naught but the Temple, as you read, ZION [i.e., the Temple] SHALL BE PLOWED AS A FIELD (Micah 3:12). Out of this argument, CAIN TURNED ON HIS BROTHER ABEL....

Judah bar Ami said: Their quarrel was about the first Eve. Said Rabbi Aibu: The first Eve had returned to dust. Then about what was their quarrel? Said Rabbi Huna: An additional twin was born with Abel, and each claimed her. The one claimed: "I will have her, because I am the firstborn"; while the other maintained: "I must have her, because she was born with me."

Questions and Commentary

Questions

1. The midrash suggests several possible reasons for the argument. What are these reasons?

2. How do the various midrashic comments attempt to support the given reasons?

3. How do you judge the quality of these explanations? Do you prefer one to another? If so, why?

Commentary

The above texts, all from *B'reishit Rabbah*, attempt to answer the basic question of what was the reason for the first act of human violence, indeed murder. I remember teaching this text at the University of Miami on the morning of September 11, 2001. When I walked into the classroom at 9:20 A.M. (eastern time), a student was speaking about the airplane crash into the World Trade Center. No one suspected it was terrorism at that time. A minute later a student came in and said he had heard a second plane may have crashed as well. It still seemed hard to believe that this was an act of terror, and I made the decision to continue with the class. But first I made an announcement: If terrorism turns out to have been the motivation, then the explanation for the act of terror would be found in the following text. In other words, any act of human violence can be reflected in the following reasons.

Reasons for Human Violence

Reason 1: Material Things. The first midrash imagines Cain and Abel quarreling over real estate and movables. This is not to say that the Rabbinic author of this text actually thought they argued about such things. Rather it is the author's way of stating that violence begins when we covet the property of others or feel our property is in jeopardy. The all-too-frequent newspaper reports of high school students being killed for a pair of tennis shoes or a jacket proves this issue is as relevant today as it was two thousand years ago.

Reason 2: Religious Honor. When it comes to choosing which answer you prefer, the midrash is very generous. It is not unusual to have multiple opinions provided within one midrash. In this case, we need not accept materialism as the driving force for violence; perhaps it is religious honor. Again, there is a playful quality to the midrash. Rabbi Joshua most likely did not really believe that Cain and Abel argued over where the Temple would be built. For one thing, they wouldn't have even known about the Temple, living as they did at least twenty generations before Abraham. Second, they would have lived in what is now modern-day Iraq, far away from Jerusalem and the site of the Temple. In order to make a connection between their field and the site of the Temple, Rabbi Joshua has to "misread" the Bible, suggesting that the word "field" always refers to the Temple even when contextually this is absurd. All of this serves a purpose, however. Rabbi Joshua is able to make the point that violence can result from overvaluing religious honor. The honor of having God's special presence in your midst (and thereby excluding it from another) is taken very seriously by many religious people, and violence often follows.

Reason 3: Women. "Was this the face that launched a thousand ships?" These words of Christopher Marlowe in his play *Dr. Faustus* are declared when the protagonist sees Helen of Troy. According to tradition, her abduction was responsible for the Trojan War. Similarly, the midrash would have us believe that Cain and Abel argued about a woman, possibly the "first Eve" (not their mother), who, according to postbiblical tradition, was ejected out of the Garden of Eden for demanding equal rights with Adam. In folklore her name becomes Lilith. Once this view is rejected, it is then surmised that Abel had a twin sister and it was over her they argued. Once again, the very far-fetched notion of a twin sister (and the implied incest) is not to be taken literally. Rather, this is another way for the Rabbis to bring in a third reason for violence: jealousy and love.

These three explanations remind us that human violence and issues of war and peace do not change over the centuries. The basic matters of jealousy, resentment, and (misplaced) religious passion still dictate our behavior, even if slight adjustments are made to account for modern realities (e.g., jingoism instead of religious chauvinism).

In order to understand the challenges of peace we must begin by understanding the motivations for war. It is astounding how little has changed with regard to motivation. Century after century, the reasons remain the same: power struggles, ethnic strife, differences in political ideology, the desire for political independence. It is only the technology that changes.

What Do You Think?

General History

Choose a war that has taken place in the twentieth century, such as World War II. What started the war? Was it for possessions? For honor? Is war ever justified for these reasons? Are these the reasons behind 9/11, or do you think there were other reasons?

Israeli History

Consider the wars of Israel's past, such as the 1948 War of Independence and the Six-Day War, up until today's reality. Is it possible to identify what started the war? Possessions? Honor? Something else?

Additional Texts

1. War, it seems, is the product of political goals, social needs, ideological commitments, and psychological frustrations. While the actual cause of a war may be most profitably sought in terms of political and economic pressures and interests, it is also clear that the prospects of war feed on an ever-ready undercurrent of psychological needs. So long as we blithely ignore how we as a society (and as a planet) discourage people from examining their own fears and asserting their belongingness and security in healthful ways, so long as we permit governments to militarize our anxieties and allow the media to glorify violence as the truest expression of adult independence, we will be trapped into a world in which aggression appears to be "natural."

Bradley Shavit Artson, *Love Peace and Pursue Peace:*
A Jewish Response to War and Nuclear Annihilation
(New York: United Synagogue of America, 1988), p. 28

2. The wars of the Greeks and the barbarians... have all flowed from one source, greed, the desire of money, glory, or pleasure, for it is on these that the human race goes mad.

Philo, *Decalogue*, 28

CHAPTER TWO

Milchemet Chovah: Required Wars

Jewish tradition divides wars into three basic categories: required wars; optional wars, in need of authorization; and commanded wars (meaning defensive).

A "required war" refers to a war fought against enemies specifically designated by God in the Bible. This list is as short as it is nonnegotiable. Included on this list are the seven Canaanite nations who were dwelling in the Land of Israel when Joshua led the Israelites into the Promised Land. The other nation on the list are the Amalekites, who attacked the Israelites from behind, shortly after they left Egypt.

Text

Deuteronomy 7:1–2

כִּי יְבִיאֲךָ֙ יְהֹוָ֣ה אֱלֹהֶ֔יךָ אֶל־הָאָ֕רֶץ אֲשֶׁר־אַתָּ֥ה בָא־ ¹
שָׁ֖מָּה לְרִשְׁתָּ֑הּ וְנָשַׁ֣ל גּוֹיִם־רַבִּ֣ים ׀ מִפָּנֶ֗יךָ הַחִתִּי֩

וְהַגִּרְגָּשִׁי וְהָאֱמֹרִי וְהַכְּנַעֲנִי וְהַפְּרִזִּי וְהַחִוִּי וְהַיְבוּסִי
שִׁבְעָה גוֹיִם רַבִּים וַעֲצוּמִים מִמֶּךָּ: ²וּנְתָנָם יְהֹוָה
אֱלֹהֶיךָ לְפָנֶיךָ וְהִכִּיתָם הַחֲרֵם תַּחֲרִים אֹתָם לֹא־
תִכְרֹת לָהֶם בְּרִית וְלֹא תְחָנֵּם:

1. When the Eternal your God brings you to the land
    that you are about to enter and possess, and [God]
    dislodges many nations before you—the Hittites,
    Girgashites, Amorites, Canaanites, Perizzites, Hivites,
    and Jebusites, seven nations much larger than you—
2. and the Eternal your God delivers them to you and
    you defeat them, you must doom them to destruc-
    tion: grant them no terms and give them no quarter.

Deuteronomy 25:17–19

¹⁷זָכוֹר אֵת אֲשֶׁר־עָשָׂה לְךָ עֲמָלֵק בַּדֶּרֶךְ בְּצֵאתְכֶם
מִמִּצְרָיִם: ¹⁸אֲשֶׁר קָרְךָ בַּדֶּרֶךְ וַיְזַנֵּב בְּךָ כָּל־הַנֶּחֱשָׁלִים
אַחֲרֶיךָ וְאַתָּה עָיֵף וְיָגֵעַ וְלֹא יָרֵא אֱלֹהִים: ¹⁹וְהָיָה
בְּהָנִיחַ יְהֹוָה אֱלֹהֶיךָ ׀ לְךָ מִכָּל־אֹיְבֶיךָ מִסָּבִיב בָּאָרֶץ
אֲשֶׁר יְהֹוָה־אֱלֹהֶיךָ נֹתֵן לְךָ נַחֲלָה לְרִשְׁתָּהּ תִּמְחֶה אֶת־
זֵכֶר עֲמָלֵק מִתַּחַת הַשָּׁמָיִם לֹא תִּשְׁכָּח:

17. Remember what Amalek did to you on your journey, after you left Egypt—

18. how, undeterred by fear of God, he surprised you on the march, when you were famished and weary, and cut down all the stragglers in your rear.

19. Therefore, when the Eternal your God grants you safety from all your enemies around you, in the land that the Eternal your God is giving you as a hereditary portion, you shall blot out the memory of Amalek from under heaven. Do not forget!

Questions and Commentary

Questions

1. How could you explain God's command to the Israelites to completely wipe out the inhabitants of Canaan? What might happen if they were allowed to survive? How does one choose between fidelity to God and the wholesale destruction of a people and their way of life?

2. How do we reconcile the aggressive behavior expected of the Israelites with the compassionate teachings more commonly associated with God? Why might later views of God be more focused on God's compassionate, non-warring characteristics?

3. What was the transgression of Amalek, and why does it merit eternal vigilance against this people?

4. How can the Israelites "blot out" the remembrance of Amalek by never forgetting what they did to the Israelites? Are there specific rituals Jews traditionally have observed in order to "blot out" the memory?

Commentary

Required war implies there is no choice but to fight. As a religious tradition, the lack of choice in Israelite history was due both to pragmatic and religious concerns. Pragmatically, the Israelites had to fight in order to win land for themselves after entering the Promised Land. Religiously, they were following the command of God. The war of Israelite conquest, first led by Joshua and then continued up through the period of King David, does not make for comfortable reading by Jews today. Labels not usually associated with Jewish tradition might even be applied: jihad, crusade, genocide. To claim that the violence was necessary because "God said so" does not generally help modern Jews become more comfortable with this part of our history. Indeed, liberal Jews are justifiably disturbed by the idea that God would want us to destroy other peoples. One of the strongest tenets of liberal Jewish faith is the idea of the compassionate, caring, and universal God who compels us to live our lives in God's image, doing good in the world and helping to repair the world.

The passages above raise many questions. Were the Israelites fighting evil, or were they simply fighting over land? How would a Canaanite's testimony in a modern international war crimes court make us feel? Is our "inheritance" of the land based on the cruel mistreatment of other peoples?

Before we feel overwhelmed by guilt, there are two mitigating facts to consider: (1) The biblical account is not a modern history; its purpose is to be a religious telling of the story. This account is not necessarily meant to be read as fact, nor is it understood to be so by contemporary scholars. The intent of the Bible is to explain who the Israelite people should be, rather than provide a scientifically verifiable historical account, and therefore it is *prescriptive*, not *descriptive*. The imagined past is meant to guide future actions. Hence, it is quite possible that there was no wide-scale genocide of the Canaanites. (2) Later Jewish tradition, while not in any way casting doubt on the legitimacy of the Jewish right to the Promised Land, became far less comfortable with the violence described in the Bible. Indeed, the required wars of the Bible do not justify such violence in later periods. In fact, Rabbinic tradition declares that there no longer can be required wars, since those specific enemies no longer exist.

The technical term in the Bible associated with the wars against the seven Canaanite nations is *cherem*. It refers to the total destruction of persons and goods, and later Jewish tradition limits the category of obligatory wars to those of conquest of the Promised Land. Any additional cases were to be explicitly mentioned by God, such as the command concerning the Amalekites.

It is important to emphasize the fact that, according to ancient Rabbinic tradition, direct revelation from God ceased more than two thousand years ago. Henceforth the only means of understanding God's will is to read and interpret the Bible. This vital insight means that no additions to the list of the seven Canaanite nations and the Amalekites will be forthcoming. It is impossible to add any more recent nations to the list, even if over the centuries certain countries have merited such inclusion due to their nefarious treatment of the Jewish people.

Was the war against the Canaanites really a jihad, a term often heard today in the Islamic world? Not according to the modern understanding of the term, by which jihad means that the enemy must convert or be killed. It was a religious war, in that God commanded and the Israelites obeyed. But it was not a religious war in that the Israelites were not trying to convert the Canaanites. The Israelites saw the war as a defense against the idolatrous influences of the neighboring nations.

As uncomfortable or foreign as these texts may seem, they have an effect on Jewish life even today. Haman, the villain of the Purim story, is traditionally linked to the Amalekites. On Purim, Jews use noisemakers to "blot out" the name of Haman, whenever his name is read from the Scroll of Esther. In this way, the physical act of "blotting out" the name of the Amalekites is performed in order to fulfill the ancient command from the Book of Deuteronomy.

What Do You Think?

General History

In the 1930s, the U.S. government complained to Japan that they had no right to persecute the Chinese people. (There are estimates that up to 30 million Chinese were brutally murdered by the Japanese during this period.) In response, the Japanese government declared that the United States had no right to criticize because of its inhumane treatment of Native Americans and African Americans. Could the same charge be leveled against Jewish claims of moral leadership? Do the war commands expressed in Deuteronomy eclipse any ethical claims later made by the Jewish people?

Israeli History

According to Jewish tradition, there are no longer any Canaanite nations or Amalekites left to fight. Therefore, in a strict sense, there can no longer be any obligatory wars. Nonetheless, do some of Israel's wars fit the rubric of obligatory war? Which ones would they be? The 1948 War of Independence? The 1956 Sinai Campaign? The Six-Day War? The Yom Kippur War? The Lebanon War? (See "Background: Reasons for War" for details about these wars.)

> *In particular, is it valid for Jews to identify their contemporary enemies (such as Hitler or Saddam Hussein, who sent missiles against Israel during Gulf War I) with Amalek?*

Additional Texts

1. Maimonides, *Sefer HaMitzvot* 187

וַאֲנַחְנוּ מְצֻוִּים לְחַטֵּט אַחֲרֵיהֶם וּלְרָדְפָם בְּכָל דּוֹר וָדוֹר עַד שֶׁיִּכְלוּ וְלֹא יִשָּׁאֵר מֵהֶן אִישׁ, וְכֵן עָשִׂינוּ עַד אֲשֶׁר תַּמּוּ וְנִכְרְתוּ בִּימֵי דָוִד וְנִתְפַּזְּרוּ הַנִּשְׁאָרִים וְנִתְעָרְבוּ בָּאֻמּוֹת עַד שֶׁלֹּא נִשְׁאַר בָּהֶם שֹׁרֶשׁ.

We are commanded to root them [the seven nations] out and pursue them throughout all generations until they are destroyed completely. This we did until their destruction was completed by David, and this remnant was scattered and intermingled with the other nations, so that no trace of them remains.

2. Rabbi Martin Weiner of San Francisco, outgoing president of the Reform movement's rabbinical union, the Central

Conference of American Rabbis, used Shabbat Zachor to draw a line from Amalek to Hitler to Saddam. A modern-day Amalek, Saddam has attacked four of his neighbors, gassed tens of thousands of his own people and pays stipends to suicide bombers, Weiner said, so "it's terribly important to remove him." Last September, Weiner was among those who backed a resolution from the Reform movement's Union of American Hebrew Congregations urging a pre-emptive strike against Iraq, if Congress supported it and U.N. backing was sought.

But for Reform Rabbi Don Rossoff, of Temple B'nai Or in Morristown, N.J., Amalek casts a very different shadow. Rossoff said he has refrained from publicly sermonizing this Purim about the war, which he opposes, because he is "haunted by Baruch Goldstein, who called the Arabs Amalek." Goldstein, a doctor in an Israeli settlement near the West Bank city of Hebron, shot to death 29 Palestinians praying in Hebron's Tomb of the Patriarch on Purim Day in 1994. Saddam is "a tyrannical, murderous dictator" who "would probably wipe out Israel if he could," Rossoff added. "But he's not the only one around. His name just starts with 'H,'" like Haman.

Joe Berkofsky, "For rabbis, it's no coincidence war on Iraq again linked to Purim," Jewish Telegraphic Agency, March 18, 2003

3. Discussions about the nature of the command for perpetual war against Amalek are not merely academic. Within the

Purim story itself, the Jews appear to understand the divine grace that brings about the fall of Haman as permission for a large-scale massacre of an entire people, along the lines envisioned in . . . Deuteronomy. Even more disturbingly, in contemporary times, some Jews have characterized the Palestinians as modern-day representations of Amalek. Last year, a prominent lawyer suggested that the biblical imperative to wipe out Amalek allows the execution of families of suicide bombers. It is no accident that Baruch Goldstein chose Purim for his 1994 massacre of Palestinians praying in a mosque. Defining the Palestinians as Amalek has allowed some to justify any attack on this people. Even as we reject out of hand the equation of Amalek with any contemporary people, we are compelled to reinterpret the troubling commandment for perpetual war against Amalek in such a way as to preclude using the text to incite violence.

Rabbi Jill Jacobs, director of outreach and education
for the Jewish Council on Urban Affairs in Chicago,
www.SocialAction.com, March 13, 2003, run by Jewish
Family & Life!

CHAPTER THREE

Milchemet R'shut: Optional Wars

The Rabbis of the Talmud tried to differentiate between different kinds of wars. The Babylonian Talmud offers the following statements regarding the difference between required and optional wars.

Text

Babylonian Talmud, *Sanhedrin* 20b

וּמוֹצִיא לְמִלְחֶמֶת הָרְשׁוּת עַל פִּי בֵּית דִּין שֶׁל שִׁבְעִים
וְאֶחָד, וּפוֹרֵץ לַעֲשׂוֹת לוֹ דֶרֶךְ, וְאֵין מְמַחֶה בְּיָדוֹ. דֶּרֶךְ
הַמֶּלֶךְ אֵין לוֹ שִׁיעוּר. וְכָל הָעָם בּוֹזְזִין וְנוֹתְנִין לוֹ, וְהוּא
נוֹטֵל חֵלֶק בְּרֹאשׁ.

He [the king] may lead forth [the army] to a voluntary war on the decision of a court of seventy-one. He may force a way through private property and none may oppose him. There is no limitation to the king's way. The plunder taken by the people [in war] must be given to him, and he receives the first choice [when it is divided].

The Rabbinic view toward optional wars was summarized by Moses Maimonides in his classic code of Jewish law, entitled the *Mishneh Torah.*

Moses Maimonides, *Mishneh Torah,* "Laws of Kings and Their Wars," 5:1–3, 6

¹אֵין הַמֶּלֶךְ נִלְחָם תְּחִלָּה אֶלָּא מִלְחֶמֶת מִצְוָה. וְאֵי זוֹ הִיא מִלְחֶמֶת מִצְוָה? זוֹ מִלְחֶמֶת שִׁבְעָה עֲמָמִים, וּמִלְחֶמֶת עֲמָלֵק, וְעֶזְרַת יִשְׂרָאֵל מִיַּד צַר שֶׁבָּא עֲלֵיהֶם; וְאַחַר־כָּךְ נִלְחָם בְּמִלְחֶמֶת הָרְשׁוּת, וְהִיא הַמִּלְחָמָה שֶׁנִּלְחָם עִם שְׁאָר הָעַמִּים כְּדֵי לְהַרְחִיב גְּבוּל יִשְׂרָאֵל וּלְהַרְבּוֹת בִּגְדֻלָּתוֹ וְשָׁמְעוֹ. ²מִלְחֶמֶת מִצְוָה, אֵינוֹ צָרִיךְ לִטֹּל בָּהּ רְשׁוּת בֵּית־דִּין, אֶלָּא יוֹצֵא מֵעַצְמוֹ בְּכָל עֵת וְכוֹפֶה הָעָם לָצֵאת. אֲבָל מִלְחֶמֶת הָרְשׁוּת, אֵינוֹ מוֹצִיא אֶת הָעָם בָּהּ אֶלָּא עַל־פִּי בֵּית־דִּין שֶׁל שִׁבְעִים וְאֶחָד. ³וּפוֹרֵץ לַעֲשׂוֹת לוֹ דֶרֶךְ וְאֵין מְמַחִין בְּיָדוֹ. וְדֶרֶךְ

הַמֶּלֶךְ אֵין לָה שָׁעוּר, אֶלָּא כְּפִי מַה שֶׁהוּא צָרִיךְ. אֵינוֹ
מְעַקֵּם הַדְּרָכִים מִפְּנֵי כַּרְמוֹ שֶׁל זֶה אוֹ מִפְּנֵי שָׂדֵהוּ שֶׁל
זֶה, אֶלָּא הוֹלֵךְ בְּשָׁוֶה וְעוֹשֶׂה מִלְחַמְתּוֹ...6 כָּל
הָאֲרָצוֹת שֶׁכּוֹבְשִׁין יִשְׂרָאֵל בַּמֶּלֶךְ עַל־פִּי בֵית־דִּין,
הֲרֵי זֶה כִּבּוּשׁ רַבִּים, וַהֲרֵי הִיא כְּאֶרֶץ־יִשְׂרָאֵל שֶׁכָּבַשׁ
יְהוֹשֻׁעַ לְכָל דָּבָר. וְהוּא, שֶׁכָּבְשׁוּ אַחַר כִּבּוּשׁ כָּל אֶרֶץ־
יִשְׂרָאֵל הָאֲמוּרָה בַּתּוֹרָה.

1. The only time a king is allowed to initiate a war is
   when it is a required (or defensive) war. What war
   is considered required? The war against the seven
   Canaanite nations (when the Land of Israel was first
   captured in the time of Joshua), the war against
   Amalek, and a war to help Israel from the hand of a
   siege that came upon them. Afterward he can wage
   an optional war, which is a war that can be fought
   with any nation in order to enlarge the borders of
   Israel and to enhance its greatness and reputation.

2. He does not have to receive permission from the
   Court to wage an obligatory war, but he can wage it
   by himself at anytime and he can compel the nation
   to go out [to war]. He cannot, however, force the
   nation to wage an optional war unless he has the
   approval of the court of seventy-one judges.

24

3. And one may trespass in order to make roads, and
    no one may protest this behavior for the road of
    a king has no measure, in accordance to what he
    needs. He shouldn't twist the road because of
    someone's vineyard, or another's field, but rather
    everyone should be treated equally, and help him
    wage his war....

6. Any lands that the king has captured with the
    permission of the Court is considered to be a con-
    quest of the majority, and it is considered to be as
    much a part of Israel as if it were conquered by
    Joshua—but this is only after all of the Land of
    Israel that was mentioned in the Torah has been
    captured.

Responsum of Rabbi David S. Shapiro, Orthodox scholar and student of Rabbi Joseph B. Soloveitchik

The category of *milchemet reshut* [optional wars that need to
be authorized by more than just the king] includes wars against
the avowed enemies of Israel, nations that flagrantly violated
the Seven Commandments [the Noachide Laws, or basic laws
of human decency] and recognize no international obligations.
This kind of war may be declared only after the Sanhedrin of
seventy-one—the highest tribunal in Israel—the king of Israel,

and the high-priest through the Urim and Tumim [divine oracles] have given their approval. Its purpose may not be conquest, plunder, or destruction. It may be waged only for the protection of Israel and for the sanctification of the name of God, that is the imposition of the Seven Commandments. . . .

No war may be waged against a nation that has not attacked Israel, or that lives up to the fundamentals of the Universal Religion. Even Edom, Ammon, and Moab, who had throughout their history displayed hostility to Israel, were not attacked, not to speak of those nations who were not bellicose. It would seem that the *milchemet reshut* [optional war in need of authorization] was limited by the ideal boundaries of the Holy Land.

David S. Shapiro. "The Jewish Attitude towards
War and Peace," in *Israel of Tomorrow*, ed. Leo Jung
(New York: Herald Square Press, 1946), p. 237

Questions and Commentary

Questions

1. Why does the Mishnah state that the king must receive authorization from the Sanhedrin for an optional war?

2. Why does the Mishnah specifically state that the king may use private property for the war, and why is the king entitled to the plunder?

3. What makes the wars of Joshua obligatory wars? What makes the wars of King David optional?

4. In addition to the Sanhedrin, why are the High Priest and the *Urim* and *Tumim* (divine oracles) consulted?

5. According to Maimonides, the king need not consult the Sanhedrin for a required war. Why would this not have been thought necessary?

Commentary

Optional wars in Jewish tradition are treated like a necessary evil. They are necessary because it is natural for kings—even Israelite kings—to wish for more land, but they are evil because such violence is not absolutely required for the safety and security of the people. Furthermore, the people themselves will be called upon to fight and often lose their lives for the sake of the pleasure of the king. (A later chapter deals with the fact that the requirements regarding who must fight differed between required and optional wars.) In order to fight an optional war, the king must present his argument for a war before

27

the Sanhedrin, the court of seventy-one judges, which also had a legislative function.

King David, albeit a revered leader, was not allowed to build the First Temple in Jerusalem. The Bible explains that this was due to his having shed much blood and waged aggressive wars in order to conquer more land. In I Chronicles 22:8 the text declares, "And the word of the Eternal came to me, saying, 'You have shed abundant blood and have made great wars; you shall not build a house to My name, because you have shed much blood upon the earth in My sight.'" This same idea is touched on again in I Chronicles 28:3: "And God said to me, 'You shall not build a house for My name, because you have been a man of war and have shed blood.'" David's wars were not required by God, and therefore he forfeited the opportunity to be known as the builder of the Temple.

According to some authorities, the protocol for conducting an optional war included seeking permission from not only the Sanhedrin but also the *Kohein Gadol* (the High Priest) and the *Urim* and *Tumim*, the oracular device used to ascertain the will of God. Since none of these institutions existed after the destruction of the Second Temple in 70 C.E., the possibility of waging an optional war became moot. Nevertheless, in the decades following the destruction of the Second Temple, many Jews sought to overthrow Roman rule in Palestine, with disastrous results. This historical fact, along with the extinction of the institutions required to wage optional war—not to mention the end of a Jewish sovereign state—helped to shape a Jewish view that eschewed any interest in wars of aggression.

The United States provides a modern example of checks and balances between the executive branch and the legislative branch regarding going to war. The Congress, not the president, formally declares war. The president must seek the approval of Congress.

As the citation from Rabbi David S. Shapiro indicates, an additional reason for waging an optional war for which authorization was required was to fight a country that was not respecting the rights of other nations. Although the motives for such a fight may be noble, the terrible impact of any war on the Israelite nation was justifiably feared. Therefore, unless under threat of direct attack, such a war was not to be permitted.

What Do You Think?

General History

Based on what you know, would you consider the 2003 war in Iraq an optional war on the part of the United States? Was the threat against the United States great enough? How realistic is it that the United States should operate as "the world's policeman"? What about Gulf War I or the Vietnam War? What is the deciding factor for the United States in determining to go to war? Who should decide whether or not we go to war? What checks and balances (like the Sanhedrin and High Priest) are in place today? How effective are today's checks and balances in this regard?

Israeli History

In the 1980s, Israel was being attacked on a regular basis by the Palestine Liberation Organization (PLO) from their outpost in Lebanon. The attacks by the PLO were not endangering the Jewish state's existence, but they were unpleasant, especially for Israelis along the northern border. The prime minister, Menachem Begin, and the defense minister, Ariel Sharon, knew they had the power to respond with an invasion. Knowing that the war itself caused a great deal of moral anguish for the Israeli government, following the army's tacit support for a massacre by Christian Lebanese forces against Lebanese Muslims, and knowing that the PLO secured worldwide sympathy for their plight from an international media that favored them as the underdog, it is reasonable to ask, was the Lebanon War a mistake? Indeed, even without considering these factors, are optional wars ever morally justified? What is an example of a modern optional war? Of a modern required war? How would you categorize the U.N. involvement (or lack thereof) in Bosnia, Kosovo, Rwanda, and Darfur?

Additional Texts

1. The Central Conference of American Rabbis stands by Israel in its struggle for survival. The present crisis in Lebanon is the result of the role of the PLO as a terrorist organization, whose acts of violence threaten the lives of the peoples of both Israel and Lebanon. These assaults were clearly intolerable, and Israel was forced to respond so as to secure its towns and villages from bombardment and from terrorist infiltration.

We commend the United States Government for its sensitivity to the needs of the Israeli and Lebanese peoples in this situation, and we urge strongly the continuance of existing policies which offer a realistic hope for peace.

We lament the tragic loss of life on all sides in Lebanon. The horrors of war remain forever deep and abiding. The shattering of lives, limbs, and homes grieves us all. We call upon all sides to act now so as to be certain that such suffering be ended by extending the cease-fire. We urge all parties to the conflict to continue these negotiations facilitated by U.S. Ambassador Habib so as to seize the moment and to work for the formation of a strong and stable central government in Lebanon freed from the presence of all foreign troops on its soil.

The Conference urges support for efforts under Jewish and non-Jewish auspices which are now seeking funds within our communities so as to provide food, medical supplies, and shelter for the people of Lebanon who are the victims of war.

This is a time appropriate for new and far-reaching peace initiatives.

"Israel: Resolution Adopted by the CCAR
at the 93rd Annual Convention of the Central
Conference of American Rabbis, New York City,
June 27–July 1, 1982," www.ccarnet.org

2. From the Torah's exaltation of peace as a predominant social value and from the strict limitations it places upon the conduct of *milchemet reshut*, we learn a somber lesson: war is at best a necessary evil, "necessary" perhaps but "evil" all the same. This lesson in turn leads us to conclude that the Torah's permit for the king to engage in war "to increase his greatness and reputation" is a political justification of such a policy but not a *moral* justification of it.

CCAR Responsa Committee, "Preventive War,"
CCAR Responsa 5762.8, www.ccarnet.org

3. In the end, the search for alternatives to the use of force bespeaks a failure of imagination—a stark unwillingness, even after September 11, to conceive of what it means for weapons of mass destruction to fall into the hands of monstrous figures like Saddam Hussein and Osama bin Laden. In the light of this unfolding and ever more perilous reality, to choose to avoid force at all costs is to choose not the lesser but the greater evil. As one self-described reluctant hawk, Bill Keller of the *New York Times,* has put it, "In the short run, war is perilous. In the long run, peace can be a killer too." This is a fitting epitaph for the lost, and not soon to be recovered, world that gave rise to the doctrine of containment.

Robert J. Lieber, "The Folly of Containment," Commentary, April 2003, p. 21

4. The elusive search for weapons of mass destruction in Iraq and mounting questions about pre-war intelligence are prompting some liberal supporters of military intervention in Iraq to reassess their positions.

Kenneth Pollack, a former CIA analyst and National Security Council official in the Clinton administration who wrote an influential book in 2002 advocating military action against Saddam Hussein, acknowledged in an article in the current issue of *The Atlantic Monthly* that "what we have learned about Iraq's WMD programs since the fall of Baghdad leads me to conclude that the case for war with Iraq was considerably weaker than I believed beforehand."

Pollack also repeats allegations that administration officials pressured CIA analysts to produce evidence of Saddam's weapons programs and used "creative omission" to support the White House's "reckless" rush to war.

In a contribution to a debate among liberal hawks hosted by the online magazine *Slate* this week, Pollack said that in retrospect he might have advocated deterrence as much as military intervention if he were to rewrite his book today. Other participants, including journalists Thomas Friedman,

Christoper Hitchens and Fareed Zakaria, maintain that ridding the world of a source of instability in the region and a murderous dictator like Saddam Hussein transcends the WMD issue, despite the chaotic postwar conditions in Iraq and the diplomatic fallout from the invasion.

Marc Perelman, "Liberal Hawks Rethink Stance on Iraq,"
Forward, January 16, 2004

CHAPTER FOUR

Milchemet Mitzvah: Defensive Wars

As Jewish tradition developed, required wars became obsolete, because the seven nations and the Amalekites no longer existed. Optional wars also became impossible to wage, since conditions necessary to authorize such wars no longer were extant. Unfortunately, a third kind of war was still necessary to consider: defensive wars. Indeed, a useful way to consider the difference between a required war and an optional war was offered by Rabbi Judah (in the Jerusalem Talmud): "Rabbi Judah designated optional [*r'shut*] a war in which we attacked them, and obligatory [*chovah*] in which they attacked us." Actually, as Jewish tradition developed, the term for such a war became not "obligatory" (*chovah*), since this implied that God required war against a specific people. Rather, the term is "commanded" (*mitzvah*), since self-defense is considered a commandment of God. Although the actual peoples are not designated by God as eternal enemies, their direct threat to the Land of Israel and the need to defend Israel and its people make the choice to go to war obvious.

Text

Numbers 10:9

וְכִי־תָבֹאוּ מִלְחָמָה בְּאַרְצְכֶם עַל־הַצַּר הַצֹּרֵר אֶתְכֶם
וַהֲרֵעֹתֶם בַּחֲצֹצְרֹת וְנִזְכַּרְתֶּם לִפְנֵי יְהֹוָה אֱלֹהֵיכֶם
וְנוֹשַׁעְתֶּם מֵאֹיְבֵיכֶם:

When you are at war in your land against an aggressor
who attacks you, you shall sound short blasts on the
trumpets, that you may be remembered before the
Eternal your God and be delivered from your enemies.

Babylonian Talmud, *Eiruvin* 45a

נָכְרִים שֶׁצָּרוּ עַל עֲיָרוֹת יִשְׂרָאֵל — אֵין יוֹצְאִין עֲלֵיהֶם
בִּכְלֵי זֵיָנָן, וְאֵין מְחַלְּלִין עֲלֵיהֶן אֶת הַשַּׁבָּת. . . . בַּמֶּה
דְּבָרִים אֲמוּרִים — כְּשֶׁבָּאוּ עַל עִסְקֵי מָמוֹן. אֲבָל בָּאוּ
עַל עִסְקֵי נְפָשׁוֹת — יוֹצְאִין עֲלֵיהֶן בִּכְלֵי זֵיָנָן, וּמְחַלְּלִין
עֲלֵיהֶן אֶת הַשַּׁבָּת. וּבְעִיר הַסְּמוּכָה לַסְּפָר, אֲפִלּוּ לֹא
בָּאוּ עַל עִסְקֵי נְפָשׁוֹת אֶלָּא עַל עִסְקֵי תֶּבֶן וָקַשׁ —
יוֹצְאִין עֲלֵיהֶן בִּכְלֵי זֵיָנָן, וּמְחַלְּלִין עֲלֵיהֶן אֶת הַשַּׁבָּת.

If gentiles besiege a Jewish city [on Shabbat], one is not allowed to go out and fight them with weapons, and one may not violate Shabbat because of the siege.... To what does this refer? Only when the goal of the siege is to appropriate possessions [but not intending to kill]. Nevertheless, if the intention of the gentiles is to kill Jews, one must go against the aggressors with weapons, and one is allowed to violate Shabbat. If the attack is on a border city, and even if the purpose was merely to take straw and stubble from them and not harm them, one is to go forth with weapons and violate Shabbat.

Questions and Commentary

Questions

1. The verse in Numbers clearly refers to a war of defense. What is the purpose of blowing trumpets?

2. According to the Talmud, what factors are necessary to allow Jews to defend themselves with weapons in violation of Shabbat? What are the specific actions that the enemy must do in order to merit violation of Shabbat by taking up arms?

3. What is the significance of the border city? What would make an attack on a border city more significant than an attack on an interior city even if there were no intent to kill its citizens? Why would this location justify breaking Shabbat?

Commentary

President John F. Kennedy was once asked how he became a hero during World War II, when he rescued the men under his command. He answered that his heroics were involuntary because "they [the Japanese] sank my boat." When it comes to finding oneself under attack, there is little choice but to fight back, unless one wants to surrender and possibly die. Jewish tradition does not consider killing in self-defense as murder, only killing. The Ten Commandments do not address the issue of killing in self-defense, only committing murder. In biblical times, any attack was met with the blowing of trumpets. The trumpet sound was for two reasons: it summoned the help of God in defense of the community, and it summoned the help of neighboring Israelite communities. Defending oneself—or coming to the aid of those in need of defense—was not seen as an option, nor was any authorization needed. It was a commandment—hence the name *milchemet mitzvah*—to fight, and even the laws of Shabbat were to be broken if lives were in danger.

The Rabbis developed a concept called *pikuach nefesh* (lit., "to save a life"), which taught that the laws of Shabbat *must* be broken if a life is in danger. As the above texts show, if property were in danger but not lives, then the command to break Shabbat did not apply. Nevertheless, if the attack was on a border city, and was therefore perhaps an ominous portent of greater attacks, then the Shabbat rules should be broken. Another explanation is that the border towns faced constant harassment from the enemy and needed to be stricter in their defense.

It is logical to understand that, of all types of war, this category is the least controversial. Jewish tradition never adopted the view that peace is preferable at all costs. Violence is a last resort, but at times the only way to fight aggressive violence is with violence. It is important to note that such wars of self-defense were responding to immediate threats and not far-off possibilities. This second notion is the subject of the next chapter.

What Do You Think?

General History

How would you categorize American involvement in the following historical wars—as required wars, optional wars, or defensive wars? Before answering, please consider an additional Jewish insight. In Leviticus 19:16, we are commanded not to stand idly by while our neighbor bleeds. According to the ancient legal midrash on this verse (Sifra), if one sees someone in danger of drowning, or being attacked by robbers, or by a wild beast, one is obligated to rescue that person. How do we balance this obligation with the need to protect our own national interests?

World War I
World War II
Vietnam War
Gulf War I
Gulf War II (Iraq War)

Israeli History

How would you categorize Israel's involvement in the following historical wars—as required wars, optional wars, or defensive wars?

1948 War of Independence
1956 Sinai Campaign
1967 Six-Day War
1973 Yom Kippur War
1982 Lebanon War

Additional Texts

1. Maimonides, *Mishneh Torah*, "Laws of Shabbat" 2:23

עוֹבְדֵי כּוֹכָבִים וּמַזָּלוֹת שֶׁצָּרוּ עַל עֲיָרוֹת יִשְׂרָאֵל, אִם בָּאוּ עַל עִסְקֵי מָמוֹן — אֵין מְחַלְּלִין עֲלֵיהֶן אֶת הַשַּׁבָּת, וְאֵין עוֹשִׂין עִמָּהֶן מִלְחָמָה. וּבְעִיר הַסְּמוּכָה לַסְּפָר — אֲפִלּוּ לֹא בָאוּ אֶלָּא עַל עִסְקֵי תֶּבֶן וָקַשׁ, יוֹצְאִין עֲלֵיהֶן בִּכְלֵי זַיִן, וּמְחַלְּלִין עֲלֵיהֶן אֶת הַשַּׁבָּת. וּבְכָל מָקוֹם, אִם בָּאוּ עַל עִסְקֵי נְפָשׁוֹת אוֹ שֶׁעָרְכוּ מִלְחָמָה אוֹ שֶׁצָּרוּ סְתָם — יוֹצְאִין עֲלֵיהֶן בִּכְלֵי זַיִן, וּמְחַלְּלִין עֲלֵיהֶן אֶת

הַשַּׁבָּת. וּמִצְוָה עַל כָּל יִשְׂרָאֵל שֶׁיְּכוֹלִין, לָבוֹא וְלָצֵאת וְלַעֲזֹר לַאֲחֵיהֶם שֶׁבְּמָצוֹר וּלְהַצִּילָם מִיַּד הָעוֹבְדֵי כּוֹכָבִים וּמַזָּלוֹת בְּשַׁבָּת; וְאָסוּר לָהֶן לְהִתְמַהְמֵהַּ לְמוֹצָאֵי שַׁבָּת. וּכְשֶׁיַּצִּילוּ אֶת אַחֵיהֶן, מֻתָּר לָהֶן לַחֲזֹר בִּכְלֵי זַיִן שֶׁלָּהֶן לִמְקוֹמָם בְּשַׁבָּת; כְּדֵי שֶׁלֹּא לְהַכְשִׁילָן לֶעָתִיד לָבוֹא.

If gentiles besieged Israelite towns, if they came for monetary reasons, it is not permitted to desecrate Shabbat on their account and we do not make war against them [on Shabbat]. In a city near the border, however, even if they came only for straw or hay, we sally forth against them with weapons and desecrate Shabbat because of them. In any location, if they came with the intention of taking lives, or if they established the lines for war, or if they simply besieged us, we sally forth against them with weapons and desecrate Shabbat because of them. It is a commandment incumbent on all Israelites who can to go out and come to the aid of their fellow Jews caught in a siege and to save them from the hand of foreigners on Shabbat, and it is forbidden to wait until Shabbat is over. And when they save their brothers, they may return with their weapons to their residences on Shabbat. [This permission is given] so that they will not be deterred [from aiding fellow Jews] in the future.

2. While Judaism does recognize the duty of a person to preserve his or her own life and defend others, it is very specific in prohibiting the shedding of innocent blood. Judaism further insists that, even in the most clear-cut case of self-defense against a precisely identified assailant, the use of excessive violence is not to be sanctioned:

> It has been taught by Rabbi Jonathan b. Saul: If one was pursuing his fellow to slay him, and the pursued could have saved himself by maiming a limb of the pursuer but instead killed his pursuer, the pursued is subject to execution on that account (*Sanhedrin* 74a).

> Al Vorspan and David Saperstein, *Jewish Dimensions
> of Social Justice: Tough Moral Choices of Our Time*
> (New York: UAHC Press, 1998), p. 169

3. The reason why a defensive war seems so awful to good people is, they esteem it to be some kind of murder: but this is a very great mistake; for it is no more murder than a legal process against a criminal. . . .

Suppose, a villain was to rob you of a valuable sum of money, and thereby expose you and your family to distress and poverty, would you not think it your duty to prosecute such a public offender? Yes, without doubt, or else you could not be a friend to the innocent part of mankind.

But suppose, he not only robs you, but in a daring manner, in your presence, murders your only son, will you not think that blood calls aloud for punishment? Surely both reason and revelation will justify you in seeking for justice in that mode by which it can be obtained. . . .

We have no choice left to us, but to submit to absolute slavery and despotism, or as free-men to stand in our own defense, and endeavor a noble resistance. Matters are at last brought to this deplorable extremity;—every reasonable method of reconciliation has been tried in vain;—our addresses to our king have been treated with neglect or contempt. . . .

David Jones, *Defensive War in a Just Cause Sinless: A Sermon Preached on the Day of the Continental Fast at Tredyffryn in Chester County* (Philadelphia: Henry Miller, 1775), pp. 16–26

4. In sum, even though the Talmud and codes do not directly connect communal self-defense to the duty of either defending oneself or intervening on behalf of another, and even though one might argue that the latter duties do not establish the former, the Talmud does not question that a community must defend itself—and even desecrate the Sabbath in the process. The codes not only endorse that right, but expand upon it. These sources also do not insist on the usual procedures required for engaging in other types of war when it is a matter of communal self-defense.

Elliot Dorff, "Defensive War," *S'Vara: A Journal of Philosophy, Law, and Judaism* 2, no. 1 (1991): 26–27

Launching a Preemptive War

Relatively speaking, the three categories of war discussed in the previous chapters are clear-cut: obligatory wars refer to those mandated in the Bible against specific enemies no longer in existence; optional wars refer to the aggressive wars of Jewish kings, also no longer possible; wars of self-defense are waged only when the enemy has invaded your land. There is another possible war, however, and its moral justification is the most difficult to assess. This is the preemptive war.

Interestingly enough, the Mishnah does not mention preemptive strikes as a possibility. It is brought up for the first time in the Babylonian Talmud, some 300 years later. The issue concerns an enemy that has yet to attack but clearly is preparing to do so. Is this considered a war that must be fought, may be fought, or should not be fought?

The problem with such questions is the interpretation of the enemy's preparations. Are they building a bomb factory that may be ready in ten years, or are there troops already amassed on the borders?

Text

Babylonian Talmud, *Sotah* 44b

אָמַר רָבָא: מִלְחָמוֹת יְהוֹשֻׁעַ לִכְבּשׁ — דִּבְרֵי הַכֹּל
חוֹבָה, מִלְחֲמוֹת בֵּית דָּוִד לִרְוָוחָה — דִּבְרֵי הַכֹּל רְשׁוּת.
כִּי פְּלִיגִי — לְמַעוּטֵי נָכְרִים דְּלָא לֵיתֵי עֲלַיְיהוּ; מָר קָרֵי
לָהּ מִצְוָה וּמָר קָרֵי רְשׁוּת.

Rava said: Everyone agrees that the wars Joshua fought to conquer [the Land of Israel] were obligatory [*chovah*]. Everyone agrees the expansionist wars of King David had to be optional [*r'shut*]. They argue about a strike against gentiles in order to weaken them from a future attack. One party considers it commanded [*mitzvah*] [in self-defense], and one requires it be optional [*r'shut*].

Questions and Commentary

Questions

1. What are the four categories of war listed in the Talmudic passage?

2. About which category do the Sages disagree?

3. What might be the reasons for the disagreement?

Commentary

When deciding to engage in a preemptive attack, the Talmud does not create a new category per se. Instead, there is a debate about whether or not the war fits into one of two preexisting categories. Is it a war of self-defense or an optional war, requiring the usual confirmation process involving the High Priest, Sanhedrin, and *Urim* and *Tumim*? Since such a confirmation process was impossible by the time of the Talmud and much of the Talmudic material is highly theoretical, labeling a war as optional was essentially calling it invalid. Therefore, only wars of self-defense can be waged. As seen in chapter 2, such wars were fought when there was an immediate threat. Indeed, there was even a distinction made between those enemies seeking possessions and those seeking to take Jewish lives, as well as the location of the fighting (i.e., border cities versus other locations). Waging a war because of a *possible* threat in future times was not considered appropriate.

What Do You Think?

General History

In World War II, the United States did not enter the war until attacked by the Japanese. Knowing what we now know about the Nazis, would the United States have been justified in declaring war prior to being attacked? Under which Jewish rubric would the United States attacking Japan and Germany fall? Required? Optional? Self-defense? Preemptive? Who should decide when a nation is justified in launching a preemptive war? The president? The legislative body?

Israeli History

Isaac ben Moses (1180–1250), an important Viennese legal scholar, in his commentary Or Zarua, argues that if there has been no enemy attack, a pre-emptive war can be waged only if the enemy has announced its intention to attack. In other words, if a hostile government declares its intention, this is seen as similar to an actual attack, and defensive measures can be taken.

Such a declaration was made by Egypt's president Gamal Nasser and Syria's president Hafiz al Assad in the months leading up to the 1967

Six-Day War. Bellicose declarations were made, such as claims they would be "freeing" Palestine and thus "liquidating" the Zionist presence. (It is important to remember that at this time, "Palestine" referred to the entire State of Israel.) Their armies were mobilized on the borders of Israel, and Nasser closed the Straits of Tiran to Israeli shipping, cutting off its only southern maritime route. Of course, Israel had to decide whether these threats were serious or not. Nevertheless, did the verbalization of such intentions give Israel a moral authority to launch its preemptive attack?

Additional Texts

1. Babylonian Talmud, *Sanhedrin* 74a

כָּל עֲבֵירוֹת שֶׁבַּתּוֹרָה אִם אוֹמְרִין לָאָדָם עֲבוֹר וְאַל
תֵּהָרֵג – יַעֲבוֹר וְאַל יֵהָרֵג, חוּץ מֵעֲבוֹדָה זָרָה וְגִילּוּי
עֲרָיוֹת וּשְׁפִיכוּת דָּמִים. . . . וּשְׁפִיכוּת דָּמִים. . . . דְּהַהוּא
דַּאֲתָא לְקַמֵּיה דְּרַבָּה, וַאֲמַר לֵיה: אֲמַר לִי מָרִי דּוּרָאי
זִיל קַטְלֵיה לִפְלָנְיָא, וְאִי לָא – קָטְלִינָא לָךְ. – אֲמַר
לֵיה: לִקְטְלוּךְ וְלָא תִּקְטוֹל. מִי יֵימַר דְּדָמָא דִּידָךְ סוּמָק
טְפֵי? דִּילְמָא דָּמָא דְּהַהוּא גַּבְרָא סוּמָק טְפֵי!

49

In every other law of the Torah, if a man is commanded, "Transgress and suffer not death," he may transgress and not suffer death, excepting idolatry, incest, and shedding blood....Murder may not be practiced to save one's life....Even as one who came before Raba and said to him, "The governor of my town has ordered me, 'Go, and kill so and so; if not, I will slay thee.'" Raba answered him, "Let him rather slay you than that you should commit murder; who knows that your blood is redder? Perhaps his blood is redder."

2. If we perceive a military strike against that nation as a case of "preventive" war, then the weight of our tradition would counsel against it. Yet it is not at all clear that this is the category we should apply in considering an attack against the Iraqi regime. Let us suppose that the arguments being made in favor of such an attack are in fact correct. Let us suppose that intelligence experts are fairly certain that Saddam Hussein's regime is building and stockpiling weapons of mass destruction. No hard evidence may exist to prove this assertion, but let us posit that the experts have good reason to believe that it is true. If this is the case, then there is also good reason to believe that this regime, which has compiled a record of aggression against other countries and against its own citizens, continues to harbor aggressive intentions. We would therefore judge Iraq to be a threat to peace and security, if not today or tomorrow then surely at some point in the realistically near future. Under these circumstances, we would be justified in viewing an attack upon Iraq as a *preemptive* war, as a strike against a real enemy engaged in the early stages of a planned military offensive, rather than as a *preventive* war against a nation that *might* one day pose a threat but which does not do so now. As we note above, a preemptive strike in the legitimate cause of self-defense more closely resembles a commanded war than a discretionary one. We deem such a strike to be morally justifiable.

CCAR Responsa Committee, "Preventive War,"
CCAR Responsa 5762.8, www.ccarnet.org

Exhortation to Fight

As we have seen, wars in ancient Jewish tradition had a religious element. Obligatory wars were required by God, as were wars of self-defense. In order to ensure the proper motivation of the people for fighting, careful consideration was paid to the words spoken to them before the battle. In addition, any exemptions of soldiers had to be properly addressed.

The Bible designates a specific official whose words prepare the troops for battle. Jewish tradition calls him the *m'shuach milchamah*, the priest who addresses the troops.

Text

Deuteronomy 20:2–4

²וְהָיָ֕ה כְּקָֽרָבְכֶ֖ם אֶל־הַמִּלְחָמָ֑ה וְנִגַּ֥שׁ הַכֹּהֵ֖ן וְדִבֶּ֥ר אֶל־הָעָֽם: ³וְאָמַ֣ר אֲלֵהֶ֗ם שְׁמַ֤ע יִשְׂרָאֵל֙ אַתֶּ֨ם קְרֵבִ֥ים הַיּ֛וֹם

לַמִּלְחָמָה עַל־אֹיְבֵיכֶם אַל־יֵרַךְ לְבַבְכֶם אַל־תִּירְאוּ
וְאַל־תַּחְפְּזוּ וְאַל־תַּעַרְצוּ מִפְּנֵיהֶם: ⁴כִּי יְהֹוָה אֱלֹהֵיכֶם
הַהֹלֵךְ עִמָּכֶם לְהִלָּחֵם לָכֶם עִם־אֹיְבֵיכֶם לְהוֹשִׁיעַ
אֶתְכֶם:

2. Before you join battle, the priest shall come forward
   and address the troops.
3. He shall say to them, "Hear, O Israel! You are about
   to join battle with your enemy. Let not your courage
   falter. Do not be in fear, or in panic, or in dread of
   them.
4. For it is the Eternal your God who marches with
   you to do battle for you against your enemy, to
   bring you victory."

Joshua 24:17–18

¹⁷כִּי יְהֹוָה אֱלֹהֵינוּ הוּא הַמַּעֲלֶה אֹתָנוּ וְאֶת־אֲבוֹתֵינוּ
מֵאֶרֶץ מִצְרַיִם מִבֵּית עֲבָדִים וַאֲשֶׁר עָשָׂה לְעֵינֵינוּ אֶת־
הָאֹתוֹת הַגְּדֹלוֹת הָאֵלֶּה וַיִּשְׁמְרֵנוּ בְּכָל־הַדֶּרֶךְ אֲשֶׁר
הָלַכְנוּ בָהּ וּבְכֹל הָעַמִּים אֲשֶׁר עָבַרְנוּ בְּקִרְבָּם: ¹⁸וַיְגָרֶשׁ
יְהֹוָה אֶת־כָּל־הָעַמִּים וְאֶת־הָאֱמֹרִי יֹשֵׁב הָאָרֶץ מִפָּנֵינוּ
גַּם־אֲנַחְנוּ נַעֲבֹד אֶת־יְהֹוָה כִּי־הוּא אֱלֹהֵינוּ:

17. For it is the Eternal our God who brought us and our fathers out of the land of Egypt, from the house of slavery, and who did those great signs in our sight, and preserved us in all the way where we went, and among all the people through whom we passed.

18. And the Eternal One drove out from before us all the people, the Amorites who live in the land; therefore will we also serve the Eternal One; for the Eternal One is our God.

Questions and Commentary

Questions

1. What is the reason for the priest declaring the words recorded in Deuteronomy 20:3–4?

2. Why should the people not be afraid?

3. Why does Joshua remind the soldiers of God's previous acts?

Commentary

It is not difficult to read into the Bible a justification of some of the morally repugnant practices of the Middle Ages and the modern period, including religious crusades and genocide. Nevertheless, the religious orientation of the ancient Israelite war of conquest—as symbolized by the exhortation of the priest—reflects a different view. While in no way justifying the horrible treatment toward the Canaanites, the job of the priest was to put the war in perspective: God required the war in order to protect the spiritual integrity of the Jewish people. This is not a battle between the Israelites and the Canaanites; it is a battle between God and the Canaanite gods, and there can be no compromise between the two radically different theologies.

This war was seen in later Jewish tradition as a unique event, never to be repeated. For one, with the end of the priesthood such a war became impossible. It was a war initiated with special divine permission, never to be issued again. It was not a war to spread religion, but rather to protect the nascent Jewish religion. The Canaanite practices to be protected against were not innocent.

They were thought to include child sacrifice, temple prostitution, and mutilation of bodies, in addition to idolatry. Fundamentally, the war was not against the Canaanite people, but rather against the Canaanite religion. This religion was seen as too dangerous to allow any compromise with it or with its adherents; hence the total ban on any survivors or surviving remnants.

What Do You Think?

General History

Is there any difference between the command to obliterate the Canaanites and the actions of Adolph Hitler against the Jews? Can the actual history of the Holocaust be compared with the literary history of the Bible? What role did religious faith play in exhorting the people to fight in both of these cases? What difference does it make, if any, if there is a religious rationale for an attack versus a political or diplomatic rationale?

Israeli History

Ultra-Orthodox Jews are exempt from serving in Israel's army and are not expected to fight in any war. Does this position seem logical? What might be the rationale for such a situation? Is there any scenario imaginable in which the ultra-Orthodox might choose to fight?

Additional Texts

1. Maimonides, *Mishneh Torah*, "Laws of Kings and Their Wars" 7:15

וְכָל הַנִּלְחָם בְּכָל לִבּוֹ לְבּוֹ פַחַד, וְתִהְיֶה כַוָּנָתוֹ לְקַדֵּשׁ אֶת הַשֵּׁם בִּלְבָד — מֻבְטָח לוֹ שֶׁלֹּא יִמְצָא נֶזֶק וְלֹא תַגִּיעֵהוּ רָעָה, וְיִבְנֶה לוֹ בַּיִת נָכוֹן בְּיִשְׂרָאֵל, וְיִזְכֶּה לוֹ וּלְבָנָיו עַד עוֹלָם, וְיִזְכֶּה לְחַיֵּי הָעוֹלָם הַבָּא. . . .

He who fights with all his heart, without fear, with the sole intention of *Kiddush HaShem* [glorifying God], is assured that no harm will befall him and no evil will overtake him. He will build for himself a lasting house in Israel, acquiring it for himself and his children forever, and will prove worthy of life in the world-to-come. . . .

2. Callinus, "Exhortation to Battle" (seventh century B.C.E.)

How long will ye slumber? when will ye take heart
And fear the reproach of your neighbors at hand?
Fie! comrades, to think ye have peace for your part,
Whilst the sword and the arrow are wasting our land!
Shame! grasp the shield close! cover well the bold breast!
Aloft raise the spear as ye march on your foe!
With no thought of retreat, with no terror confessed,
Hurl your last dart in dying, or strike your last blow.

Oh, 'tis noble and glorious to fight for our all,—
For our country, our children, the wife of our love!
Death comes not the sooner; no soldier shall fall,
Ere his thread is spun out by the sisters above.
Once to die is man's doom; rush, rush to the fight!
He cannot escape, though his blood were Jove's own.
For a while let him cheat the shrill arrow by flight;
Fate will catch him at last in his chamber alone.
Unlamented he dies;—unregretted. Not so,
When, the tower of his country, in death falls the brave;
Thrice hallowed his name amongst all, high or low,
As with blessings alive, so with tears in the grave.

Callinus, "Exhortation to Battle," trans. Henry Nelson
Coleridge, in *Greek Poets in English Verse*, ed. William
Hyde Appleton (New York: Houghton Mifflin, 1893),
pp. 112–113

CHAPTER SEVEN

Military Exemptions

The question of who fights in Jewish wars concerns more than the practical expectations of various Jewish soldiers. Central to the issue is the understanding of the need for the war in the first place. Military exemptions in one type of war may not be allowed in another. Furthermore, the reason for the exemptions reflect the general Jewish view not only toward war but also regarding the very purpose of life.

Text

Deuteronomy 20:5–8

וְדִבְּר֣וּ הַשֹּׁטְרִים֮ אֶל־הָעָם֮ לֵאמֹר֒ מִֽי־הָאִ֞ישׁ אֲשֶׁ֨ר בָּנָ֤ה

בַֽיִת־חָדָשׁ֙ וְלֹ֣א חֲנָכ֔וֹ יֵלֵ֖ךְ וְיָשֹׁ֣ב לְבֵית֑וֹ פֶּן־יָמוּת֙

בַּמִּלְחָמָ֔ה וְאִ֥ישׁ אַחֵ֖ר יַחְנְכֶֽנּוּ׃ ⁶וּמִֽי־הָאִ֞ישׁ אֲשֶׁ֨ר נָטַ֤ע

כֶּרֶם וְלֹא חִלְּלוֹ יֵלֵךְ וְיָשֹׁב לְבֵיתוֹ פֶּן־יָמוּת בַּמִּלְחָמָה
וְאִישׁ אַחֵר יְחַלְּלֶנּוּ: 7וּמִי־הָאִישׁ אֲשֶׁר אֵרַשׂ אִשָּׁה וְלֹא
לְקָחָהּ יֵלֵךְ וְיָשֹׁב לְבֵיתוֹ פֶּן־יָמוּת בַּמִּלְחָמָה וְאִישׁ אַחֵר
יִקָּחֶנָּה: 8וְיָסְפוּ הַשֹּׁטְרִים לְדַבֵּר אֶל־הָעָם וְאָמְרוּ מִי־
הָאִישׁ הַיָּרֵא וְרַךְ הַלֵּבָב יֵלֵךְ וְיָשֹׁב לְבֵיתוֹ וְלֹא יִמַּס
אֶת־לְבַב אֶחָיו כִּלְבָבוֹ:

5. Then the official shall address the troops, as follows:
   "Is there anyone who has built a new house but has
   not dedicated it? Let him go back to his home, lest
   he die in battle and another dedicate it.

6. Is there anyone who has planted a vineyard but has
   never harvested it? Let him go back to his home, lest
   he die in battle and another harvest it.

7. Is there anyone who paid the bride-price for a wife
   but has not yet married her? Let him go back to his
   home, lest he die in battle and another marry her."

8. The official shall go on addressing the troops and
   say, "Is there anyone afraid and disheartened? Let
   him go back to his home, lest the courage of his
   comrades flag like his."

The Book of Deuteronomy thus delineates a list of exemptions
from military battle. The list included in verses 5–7 could
be described as domestic, dealing with the enjoyment of a

house, a vineyard, and a wife. The issue, however, is not simply one of enjoyment; it also relates to completion. In each instance, the prospective soldier has "unfinished business" waiting at home.

The reason given in verse 8, though, is different. This reason deals with the fears of the soldiers, and there have been many commentaries concerning the real meaning of this category.

Nachmanides (1194–1270) on Deuteronomy 20:8

וְעַל דַּעַת רַבִּי עֲקִיבָא הוּא כְּמַשְׁמָעוֹ, כִּי מִי שֶׁיִּרָא אַחַר הַבְטָחַת הַכֹּהֵן אֵינֶנּוּ בּוֹטֵחַ בַּה׳ כָּרָאוּי וְלֹא יַעֲשֶׂה לוֹ הַנֵּס. וְטַעַם "וְרַךְ הַלֵּבָב", שֶׁאֵינוֹ בְּטִבְעוֹ לִרְאוֹת מַכַּת חֶרֶב וְהֶרֶג כִּי "הַיָּרֵא" הוּא אֲשֶׁר לֹא יִבְטַח, וְיַחֲזִיר אוֹתוֹ מִפְּנֵי מִעוּט בִּטְחוֹנוֹ, וְ"רַךְ הַלֵּבָב" מִפְּנֵי חֲלֹשׁ טִבְעוֹ, כִּי יָנוּס אוֹ יִתְעַלָּף.

According to Rabbi Akiva, who says that "afraid and disheartened" means what it says, for anyone who is afraid after the priest has given assurance does not truly trust God, and no miracles will be performed for him. The rationale for exempting the one who is disheartened is that it is not in his nature to see the fury of the sword and the slaughter. The one who is "afraid" is one who has no faith, and he should be returned because of his lack of faith. The one who is "disheartened" is returned because of his delicate nature—for he will flee, or faint.

Rabbi Chizkiya ben Manoach (Chizkuni, Twelfth Century) on Deuteronomy 20:8

מִי הָאִישׁ הַיָּרֵא – לִסְבֹּל מַכַּת אֲחֵרִים.

וְרַךְ הַלֵּבָב – לְהַכּוֹת אֲחֵרִים.

Is there anyone afraid?—to endure the blows of others. And disheartened?—to smite others.

Mishnah Sotah 8:7

בַּמֶּה דְבָרִים אֲמוּרִים, בְּמִלְחֶמֶת הָרְשׁוּת. אֲבָל בְּמִלְחֶמֶת מִצְוָה, הַכֹּל יוֹצְאִין, אֲפִלּוּ חָתָן מֵחֶדְרוֹ וְכַלָּה מֵחֻפָּתָהּ. אָמַר רַבִּי יְהוּדָה, בַּמֶּה דְבָרִים אֲמוּרִים, בְּמִלְחֶמֶת מִצְוָה. אֲבָל בְּמִלְחֶמֶת חוֹבָה, הַכֹּל יוֹצְאִין, אֲפִלּוּ חָתָן מֵחֶדְרוֹ וְכַלָּה מֵחֻפָּתָהּ.

62

To what do [these exemptions] refer? Optional wars. But in the case of a commanded war [i.e., self-defense], all go out [to fight], even the groom from his chuppah and the bride from her chuppah. Rabbi Judah said: To what do [these exemptions] refer? Wars of self-defense. But in an obligatory war [i.e., against the seven nations or the Amalekites], all go out [to fight], even the groom from his chuppah and the bride from her chuppah.

Questions and Commentary

Questions

1. Concerning the "domestic" reasons given for the exemptions, what is the logic behind not involving such soldiers?

2. What is a crucial difference between the domestic reasons and the fear/disheartened reasons?

3. According to Nachmanides, what is the difference between "afraid" and "disheartened"? Why do both release the person from fighting?

4. According to Chizkuni, what is the difference between the two terms?

5. In *Mishnah Sotah*, the anonymous opinion argues that exemptions are only for optional wars, not obligatory ones. According to Rabbi Judah, all fight when it is an obligatory war, but exemptions are allowed for wars of self-defense. Which of the two positions makes more sense?

Commentary

Exemptions in war are delineated in the Bible and therefore must be taken seriously by later authorities. Nevertheless, logic dictates that in cases of divine mandate, or self-defense, no exemptions can exist. If God clearly requires the war, or if your country is under attack, then the option to stay home is absurd. Certainly the idea of enjoying one's honeymoon while the homestead is under attack is ludicrous. It is more understandable—although not necessarily excusable—that a soldier might not want to fight in an obligatory war commanded by God. This actually occurred in the Bible when some of the tribes wanted to stay on the eastern side of the Jordan and not fight the Canaanites (Numbers 32). Moses refused them, declaring they had to fight first and then return to their homes. If the issue had been one of self-defense, the question would never have been raised.

It is also clear that citizen soldiers would rather be enjoying their home life than fighting an optional war for the pleasure of the king. The Mishnah's interpretation of the exemptions (the anonymous opinion at the beginning) allows a fair number of soldiers to leave the field in such a war. Any king wanting to wage an optional war will know he cannot count on a full citizen army. This too would be seen by the ancient Rabbis as a positive deterrent against a king's waging an irresponsible war.

A crucial difference between the domestic reasons and the reasons of fear or being disheartened involves proof of one's situation. A recently married man can furnish proof. Likewise a house is either built or not. But how can one determine the amount of fear experienced by a soldier, for who can see the inner workings of the mind of another? Who can stop anyone not willing to fight from saying he does not have the courage? In matters of national defense, there is no need to ask, and in matters of optional wars, the loophole is glaring. Once again, no Israelite king could effectively wage war without the passionate consent of his people.

There was another option open to kings: the mercenary force. The Book of Deuteronomy, which takes place before the settlement of Canaan but was actually written centuries later during the monarchy, looks back to an earlier, idealistic time when wars were fought by citizen soldiers, and not by hirelings of the king.

In our modern age, there is another category to consider: conscientious objectors. The category of conscientious objectors became a status to consider carefully particularly during the draft for the Vietnam War. Can a Jew be a conscientious objector, according to Jewish interpretation of our ancient texts? According to Title I of the Universal Military Training and Service Act:

> Nothing contained in this title shall be construed to require any person to be subject to combatant training and service in the armed forces of the United States who, by reason of religious training and belief, is conscientiously opposed to participation in war in any form. Religious training and belief in this connection means an individual's belief in a relation to a Supreme Being involving duties superior to those arising from any human relation, but does not include essentially political, sociological, or philosophical views or merely personal moral code.

Whether Jewish "religious training and belief" enabled one to avoid serving in a war with which one disagreed became a critical question in the Vietnam era as never before.

What Do You Think?

General History

During the Vietnam War, many Americans chose not to serve and declared themselves conscientious objectors. Can one be a selective conscientious objector, based on the particular war, or is it an "all-or-nothing" classification, wherein if you are against one war you are against all wars? What do you think would be the opinion of most governments? Some Jewish conscientious objectors have cited the interpretation of "disheartened" from Deuteronomy 20:8 as a Jewish religious justification for pacifism. Should the draft board, which required a religious objection as criteria for a conscientious objector exemption, have granted an exemption to such Jews?

Israeli History

If one argues that the U.S. war in Vietnam was not a war of self-defense but rather an optional war of aggression, then does it follow that someone refusing to serve should not be condemned? What about officers in the Israel Defense Forces who, during the second intifada, refused to serve in the West Bank, in effect declaring the operations there an optional war?

Additional Texts

1. *Mishnah Sotah* 8:6

וְהָיָה כְּכַלֹּת הַשֹּׁטְרִים לְדַבֵּר אֶל הָעָם וּפָקְדוּ שָׂרֵי
צְבָאוֹת בְּרֹאשׁ הָעָם, וּבַעֲקֵבוֹ שֶׁל עָם. מַעֲמִידִין זְקִיפִין
לִפְנֵיהֶם, וַאֲחֵרִים מֵאֲחוֹרֵיהֶם, וְכַשִׁילִין שֶׁל בַּרְזֶל
בִּידֵיהֶן, וְכָל הַמְבַקֵּשׁ לַחֲזוֹר, הָרְשׁוּת בְּיָדוֹ לְקַפֵּחַ אֶת
שׁוֹקָיו, שֶׁתְּחִלַּת נִיסָה נְפִילָה, שֶׁנֶּאֱמַר (שׁ"א ד) נָס
יִשְׂרָאֵל לִפְנֵי פְלִשְׁתִּים וְגַם מַגֵּפָה גְדֹלָה הָיְתָה בָעָם,
וּלְהַלָּן הוּא אוֹמֵר (שם לא) וַיָּנֻסוּ אַנְשֵׁי יִשְׂרָאֵל מִפְּנֵי
פְלִשְׁתִּים וַיִּפְּלוּ חֲלָלִים וְגוֹ':

WHEN THE OFFICIALS HAVE FINISHED ADDRESSING THE TROOPS,
ARMY COMMANDERS SHALL ASSUME COMMAND OF THE TROOPS
(Deuteronomy 20:9). The leaders of the legions are at the
head of the people and at the rear. Soldiers would stand
in front of them and behind them, and they had iron
axes in their hands. Anyone who wished to return, the
commander was permitted to bend his legs, for retreat
begins with falling, as it is written: ISRAEL FLED FROM THE
PHILISTINES AND THERE WAS A GREAT PLAGUE AMONG THE
PEOPLE (I Samuel 4). Later it says: THE PEOPLE OF ISRAEL
FLED FROM THE PHILISTINES AND MANY FELL…(I Samuel 31).

2. The Associated Press, "Israeli Soldiers Refuse to Serve in West Bank"

JERUSALEM—About a dozen reservists from the Israeli army's top commando unit declared Sunday they would no longer serve in the West Bank and Gaza Strip, reflecting growing unease with Israel's hard-fisted policy in the Palestinian areas.

Thirteen reservists, including three officers, from "Sayeret Matkal" made their declaration in a letter to Prime Minister Ariel Sharon, according to Israeli media.

"We cannot continue to stand silent," they wrote, charging that Israeli military activities in the West Bank and Gaza Strip are depriving "millions of Palestinians of human rights" and endangering "the fate of Israel as a democratic, Zionist and Jewish country."

"Sayeret Matkal" is the top commando unit in the Israeli military and its most prestigious. Ex-Prime Minister Ehud Barak was once its commander, and another former premier, Benjamin Netanyahu, also served in the force, known for daring operations outside Israel's borders. Its soldiers rarely serve in the Palestinian areas.

Sharon's office had no immediate comment. A military spokesman released a one-sentence statement criticizing the soldiers for "using their uniforms and the name of the unit where they serve as a lever for publicizing their political views." The military would not respond to a question of how many reservists serve in the "Sayeret Matkal."

More than three years of Palestinian-Israeli violence has stretched nerves thin among Israelis and further fractured the consensus over the military, once the unquestioned pinnacle of Israeli society.

St. Petersburg Times, December 23, 2003

3. There is a loophole in the war legislation, a loophole so gaping that it allows those not convinced of the validity of the war to reassert their sovereignty through legal shenanigans. Doubts about the validity of the war will stir up their own social momentum and induce many to seek wholesale exemptions. The result is a war declared by the executive and approved by the Sanhedrin, which sputters for failing to persuade the populace of its necessity.

Mobilization cannot succeed without a high degree of popular motivation. Many will express their half-heartedness by dragging their feet in the hope of being, as the Talmud says, "The last to go to war and the first to return." By expressing their reluctance to fight, the populace retains a semblance of sovereignty, and indirectly passes judgment on whether the military venture is both necessary and serves legitimate political ends.

The upshot is that mandatory and discretionary wars both require a moral and a political base. Otherwise, the war effort threatens to be undermined by the morale of that community which constitutes the resource of power. David Ben-Gurion summed it up well when he said, "Two-thirds of military prowess is popular morale."

Reuven Kimelman, *Proceedings of the Rabbinical Assembly* 49 (1987)

CHAPTER EIGHT

The Treatment of Prisoners of War

Warfare itself is always cruel, and the biblical view of war especially harsh. Nevertheless, in the Bible itself—and even more in later Rabbinic tradition—the severity of war was tempered by rules that were far more humane than those found in other contemporary cultures. Some of these rules specifically relate to the treatment of prisoners of war.

In modern times, when it comes to prisoners of war, there are internationally accepted regulations, the most famous being the Geneva Convention. This code, adopted in 1949, declares, among other things:

> Persons taking no active part in the hostilities, including members of armed forces who have laid down their arms and those placed hors de combat by sickness, wounds, detention, or any other cause, shall in all circumstances be treated humanely, without any adverse distinction founded on race, color, religion or faith, sex, birth or wealth, or any other similar criteria.

Unfortunately, it has not been common practice among warring peoples to follow the kinds of guidelines mentioned in this code. Certainly, the approach of the Geneva Convention was not reflected in the practice of the Nazis and Japanese in World War II, nor was it always followed by the Allies. When American soldiers fought Native Americans and later each other in the Civil War, numerous atrocities against unarmed soldiers were committed.

It is all the more remarkable then that Jewish texts dating thousands of years old would reflect a humane approach toward prisoners. Consider this example:

אִם־רָעֵב שֹׂנַאֲךָ הַאֲכִלֵהוּ לָחֶם וְאִם־צָמֵא הַשְׁקֵהוּ
מָיִם:

If your enemy be hungry, give him bread to eat; and if he is thirsty, give him water to drink.

Proverbs 25:21

This is not to suggest that the Bible does not condone killing prisoners. As shown in chapter 2, the biblical tradition is quite harsh concerning certain nations. However, there are more liberal expectations also expressed in the Bible. This section from Deuteronomy reflects the complicated Jewish approach toward the treatment of prisoners.

Text

Deuteronomy 20:10–14

10 כִּי־תִקְרַב אֶל־עִיר לְהִלָּחֵם עָלֶיהָ וְקָרָאתָ אֵלֶיהָ
לְשָׁלוֹם: 11 וְהָיָה אִם־שָׁלוֹם תַּעַנְךָ וּפָתְחָה לָךְ וְהָיָה
כָּל־הָעָם הַנִּמְצָא־בָהּ יִהְיוּ לְךָ לָמַס וַעֲבָדוּךָ: 12 וְאִם־לֹא
תַשְׁלִים עִמָּךְ וְעָשְׂתָה עִמְּךָ מִלְחָמָה וְצַרְתָּ עָלֶיהָ:
13 וּנְתָנָהּ יְהוָה אֱלֹהֶיךָ בְּיָדֶךָ וְהִכִּיתָ אֶת־כָּל־זְכוּרָהּ
לְפִי־חָרֶב: 14 רַק הַנָּשִׁים וְהַטַּף וְהַבְּהֵמָה וְכֹל אֲשֶׁר
יִהְיֶה בָעִיר כָּל־שְׁלָלָהּ תָּבֹז לָךְ וְאָכַלְתָּ אֶת־שְׁלַל
אֹיְבֶיךָ אֲשֶׁר נָתַן יְהוָה אֱלֹהֶיךָ לָךְ:

10. When you approach a town to attack it, you shall offer it terms of peace.
11. If it responds peaceably and lets you in, all the people present there shall serve you at forced labor.
12. If it does not surrender to you, but would join battle with you, you shall lay siege to it;
13. and when the Eternal your God delivers it into your hand, you shall put all its males to the sword.
14. You may, however, take as your booty the women, the children, the livestock, and everything in the town—all its spoil—and enjoy the use of the spoil of your enemy, which the Eternal your God gives you.

73

Questions and Commentary

The passage above deals both with prisoners of war who are soldiers and with those who are civilians. In both cases the Bible is referring to people who are not members of the seven nations that are to be completely annihilated. Instead, the Bible is dealing with members of other countries.

Questions

1. What is the first duty an advancing Israelite army is to undertake?

2. If the city surrenders, what are the Israelites supposed to do?

3. If the city does not surrender, the Israelite army puts the city under siege. What does this mean? What are the moral implications of such an action?

4. Once the city has fallen, what happens to the various people and possessions in the city? Why are distinctions made?

Commentary

Clearly the rules for warfare in Deuteronomy are not as liberal as later Rabbinic tradition will reflect. Nevertheless, there is a recognition of the basic value of human life, indicated by the very idea that terms of peace should always precede the battle. If the city chooses to fight, then its captured inhabitants are dealt with more severely.

The men—representing possible future fighters—are killed; women and children are taken as spoils. However, according to Deuteronomy 21:10–14, the captured women must be treated humanely. There is a clear sense of respect for the personhood of the captive. Obviously this approach is idealistic and therefore not always reflective of how woman captives were treated in reality, but its inclusion points to a fundamental desire in Deuteronomy, as well as in later Jewish sources, to recognize the dignity in every human being. War dehumanizes its participants. Jewish tradition attempts to preserve some humanity whenever possible.

When it comes to laying siege to the city, logic dictates that no materials, food, or water should be allowed to reach the inhabitants. Siege warfare, therefore, by definition contravenes the Geneva Convention—in spirit as well as in letter. The suffering—even starvation—of civilians is necessary for the siege to work.

The "humane" justification of a siege is that suffering now will lead to an early end to the war. This moral calculation is not unknown in our era. This question was reflected in the choice of Harry S. Truman to drop the atomic bomb on Japan, taking many lives in order to prevent hundreds of thousands more being lost should the war be prolonged.

Sifrei D'varim, the earliest midrash on Deuteronomy, suggests that one must not make a city under attack suffer starvation or thirst or die from sicknesses (on Deuteronomy 20:10). This view would make a siege impossible to effect. Perhaps for this reason later Jewish law favors incorporating a siege if it will prevent future loss of life.

What Do You Think?

General History

Can the deliberate slaughter of innocent men and women be justified because it saves the lives of other men and women? Was the dropping of the atomic bomb by President Truman justified from a pragmatic point of view? From a moral point of view?

Israeli History

The Israel Defense Forces (IDF) has an underlying philosophy of warfare entitled Toharat HaNeshech, "Purity of Arms." Read the following selection from this code. Is the code pragramtic or too idealistic? Would you be willing to follow this code?

Purity of Arms—The IDF servicemen and women will use their weapons and force only for the purpose of their mission, only to the necessary extent, and will maintain their humanity even during combat. IDF soldiers will not use their weapons and force to harm human beings who are not combatants or prisoners of war, and will do all in their power to avoid causing harm to their lives, bodies, dignity, and property.

Additional Texts

1. Maimonides, *Mishneh Torah*, "Laws of Kings and their Wars" 6:7

כְּשֶׁצָּרִין עַל עִיר לְתָפְשָׂהּ, אֵין מַקִּיפִין אוֹתָהּ מֵאַרְבַּע רוּחוֹתֶיהָ, אֶלָּא מִשָּׁלֹשׁ רוּחוֹתֶיהָ; וּמַנִּיחִין מָקוֹם לַבּוֹרֵחַ וּלְכָל מִי שֶׁיִּרְצֶה לְהִמָּלֵט עַל נַפְשׁוֹ, שֶׁנֶּאֱמַר: וַיִּצְבְּאוּ עַל מִדְיָן כַּאֲשֶׁר צִוָּה ה' אֶת משֶׁה – מִפִּי הַשְּׁמוּעָה לָמְדוּ שֶׁבְּכָךְ צִוָּהוּ.

When siege is laid to a city for the purpose of capture, it may not be surrounded on all four sides but only on three to give an opportunity for escape to those who would flee to save their lives, as it is said: "They took the field against Midian, as the Eternal had commanded Moses" (Numbers 31:7). It has been learned by tradition that that was an instruction given to Moses.

2. II Samuel 12:26–31

‏26וַיִּלָּחֶם יוֹאָב בְּרַבַּת בְּנֵי עַמּוֹן וַיִּלְכֹּד אֶת־עִיר הַמְּלוּכָה: 27וַיִּשְׁלַח יוֹאָב מַלְאָכִים אֶל־דָּוִד וַיֹּאמֶר נִלְחַמְתִּי בְרַבָּה גַּם־לָכַדְתִּי אֶת־עִיר הַמָּיִם: 28וְעַתָּה

אֶסֹף אֶת־יֶתֶר הָעָם וַחֲנֵה עַל־הָעִיר וְלָכְדָהּ פֶּן־אֶלְכֹּד
אֲנִי אֶת־הָעִיר וְנִקְרָא שְׁמִי עָלֶיהָ׃ 29 וַיֶּאֱסֹף דָּוִד אֶת־
כָּל־הָעָם וַיֵּלֶךְ רַבָּתָה וַיִּלָּחֶם בָּהּ וַיִּלְכְּדָהּ׃ 30 וַיִּקַּח אֶת־
עֲטֶרֶת־מַלְכָּם מֵעַל רֹאשׁוֹ וּמִשְׁקָלָהּ כִּכַּר זָהָב וְאֶבֶן
יְקָרָה וַתְּהִי עַל־רֹאשׁ דָּוִד וּשְׁלַל הָעִיר הוֹצִיא הַרְבֵּה
מְאֹד׃ 31 וְאֶת־הָעָם אֲשֶׁר־בָּהּ הוֹצִיא וַיָּשֶׂם בַּמְּגֵרָה
וּבַחֲרִצֵי הַבַּרְזֶל וּבְמַגְזְרֹת הַבַּרְזֶל וְהֶעֱבִיר אוֹתָם
בַּמַּלְכֵּן [בַּמַּלְבֵּן] וְכֵן יַעֲשֶׂה לְכֹל עָרֵי בְנֵי־עַמּוֹן וַיָּשָׁב
דָּוִד וְכָל־הָעָם יְרוּשָׁלָ͏ִם׃

26. Joab attacked Rabbah of Ammon and captured the royal city.
27. Joab sent messengers to David and said, "I have attacked Rabbah and I have already captured the water city.
28. Now muster the rest of the troops and besiege the city and capture it; otherwise I will capture the city myself, and my name will be connected with it."
29. David mustered all the troops and marched on Rabbah, and he attacked it and captured it.
30. The crown was taken from the head of their king and it was placed on David's head—it weighed a talent of gold, and [on it] were precious stones. He also carried off a vast amount of booty from the city.

31. He led out the people who lived there and set them to work with saws, iron threshing boards, and iron axes, or assigned them to brickmaking.

3. A. Prisoners of war, in the sense of the present Convention, are persons belonging to one of the following categories, who have fallen into the power of the enemy:

1. Members of the armed forces of a Party to the conflict as well as members of militias or volunteer corps forming part of such armed forces.

2. Members of other militias and members of other volunteer corps, including those of organized resistance movements, belonging to a Party to the conflict and operating in or outside their own territory, even if this territory is occupied, provided that such militias or volunteer corps, including such organized resistance movements, fulfill the following conditions:

   (a) That of being commanded by a person responsible for his subordinates;

   (b) That of having a fixed distinctive sign recognizable at a distance;

   (c) That of carrying arms openly;

   (d) That of conducting their operations in accordance with the laws and customs of war.

3. Members of regular armed forces who profess allegiance to a government or an authority not recognized by the Detaining Power.

4. Persons who accompany the armed forces without actually being members thereof, such as civilian members of military aircraft crews, war correspondents, supply contractors, members of labour units or of services responsible for the welfare of the armed forces, provided that they have received authorization from the armed forces which they accompany, who shall provide them for that purpose with an identity card similar to the annexed model.

5. Members of crews, including masters, pilots and apprentices, of the merchant marine and the crews of civil aircraft of the Parties to the conflict, who do not benefit by more favourable treatment under any other provisions of international law.

6. Inhabitants of a non-occupied territory, who on the approach of the enemy spontaneously take up arms to resist the invading forces, without having had time to form themselves into regular armed units, provided they carry arms openly and respect the laws and customs of war.

B. The following shall likewise be treated as prisoners of war under the present Convention:

1. Persons belonging, or having belonged, to the armed forces of the occupied country, if the occupying Power considers it necessary by reason of such allegiance to intern them, even though it has originally liberated them while hostilities were going on outside the territory it occupies, in particular

where such persons have made an unsuccessful attempt to rejoin the armed forces to which they belong and which are engaged in combat, or where they fail to comply with a summons made to them with a view to internment.

From the Geneva Convention III,
adopted on August 12th, 1949

4. Second only to the Jews, Soviet prisoners of war (POWs) were the largest group of victims of Nazi extermination policy. . . .

German policy on the Soviet POWs was made easier by the lack of clarity in the reciprocal obligations of the two countries in war, under international law. The Soviet Union had not ratified the 1929 Geneva Convention of Prisoners of War, nor had it specifically declared its commitment to the 1907 Hague Convention on the Rules of War. Both nations, therefore, were bound only by the general international law of war, as it had developed in modern times. But under that law, too, prisoners of war had to have their lives protected, and they had to be treated humanely and to receive nourishment, clothing, and housing that were on a par with those accorded to its own reserve troops by the country in which they were held.

The Reich government exploited this ambiguous situation by claiming that it was under no obligation to the Soviet Union under international law; and it had no intention of restricting itself in any way with respect to the conduct of the war, the policy it pursued in occupied territories, and its treatment of prisoners of war. It also rejected an offer made by the Soviet Union in July 1941 for mutual recognition of the Hague Convention on the Rules of War, since it was convinced that a German victory was imminent.

> *Encyclopedia of the Holocaust*, vol. 3, ed. Israel Gutman
> (New York: Simon and Schuster Macmillan, 1990),
> pp. 1192–93

5. As the scandal over U.S. abuse of Iraqi prisoners mounts, only a handful of Jewish organizations have stepped forward to speak out on the issue.

Three of the organizations—the Anti-Defamation League, the National Council for Jewish Women and the Religious Action Center of Reform Judaism—issued statements condemning the turn of events. But two groups—the Jewish War Veterans and the Jewish Institute for National Security Affairs, or Jinsa—took a different tack, reserving the bulk of their criticism for critics of the Bush administration.

Jinsa, a Washington-based organization with strong ties to several Pentagon officials, jumped to the defense of the Bush administration. In its May 11 statement, Jinsa deplored the abuse of prisoners, but argued that "it would be a far greater tragedy if it led to the resignation of Defense Secretary Donald Rumsfeld."

The Jewish veterans issued a statement titled "Show Trials Will Not Solve the Iraq Question," which declared: "In the rush to satisfy the cravings of the media—which has created frenzy in regard to the allegations of abuse—the military must not be guilty of scapegoating those enlisted personnel who are at the lowest reaches of the chain of command."

Most Jewish groups have avoided issuing statements on the controversy, including the community's two major umbrella organizations, the Jewish Council for Public Affairs and the Conference of Presidents of Major American Jewish Organizations. While both umbrella organizations are opting for silence now, they each issued statements in advance of the Iraq war supporting the use of force as a last resort to eliminate Saddam Hussein's weapons of mass destruction.

Silence on the prisoner issue is a mistake, said Rabbi David Saperstein, director of the RAC. "This is a moral and political issue that affects all Americans," Saperstein said, "and the Jewish community has an obligation to speak out when our country is involved in activities that are morally problematic."

Miriam Colton, "Prisoner Abuse Controversy Rages,
Most Groups Keep Quiet," *Forward*, May 14, 2004

6. A series of criminal abuses of Iraqi prisoners of war by United States soldiers has been discovered at the Abu Ghraib prison. Ultimate responsibility for these abuses remains to be determined, as does the nature and application of interrogation guidelines developed in the wake of September 11, 2001. Jewish tradition insists that, even in warfare, the military uphold ethical standards. Understanding war's dehumanizing effects on combatants, the great commentator Ramban warns that at such times we must be even more conscious of our moral behavior (see comment on Deuteronomy 23:10). A military investigation into the responsibility for and extent of the abuses at Abu Ghraib is ongoing. The criminal abuse of Iraqi prisoners of war involves a very few of the thousands of men and women serving in military and civilian roles in Iraq who perform their service with honor, integrity and compassion.

"Iraq: Resolution Adopted by the CCAR at the 115th Annual Convention of the Central Conference of American Rabbis, Toronto, Canada, June 2004," www.ccarnet.org

CHAPTER NINE

The Treatment of Natural Resources during War

The concept of "total war"—so prevalent in the twentieth century—implies fighting a war on all fronts and at all costs. As early as the Bible, however, Jewish tradition set limits on the range of acceptable behavior. For instance, the dignity of a female captive had to be observed—a ludicrous notion for most invading armies even today. Another critical example concerns the treatment of the natural resources of the battle area. As we will see, the Jewish sources are adamant supporters of ecological preservation, even during the trauma of war.

Text
Deuteronomy 20:19–20

כִּי־תָצוּר אֶל־עִיר יָמִים רַבִּים לְהִלָּחֵם עָלֶיהָ לְתָפְשָׂהּ 19
לֹא־תַשְׁחִית אֶת־עֵצָהּ לִנְדֹּחַ עָלָיו גַּרְזֶן כִּי מִמֶּנּוּ תֹאכֵל

וְאֹתוֹ לֹא תִכְרֹת כִּי הָאָדָם עֵץ הַשָּׂדֶה לָבֹא מִפָּנֶיךָ בַּמָּצוֹר: ²⁰רַק עֵץ אֲשֶׁר־תֵּדַע כִּי לֹא־עֵץ מַאֲכָל הוּא אֹתוֹ תַשְׁחִית וְכָרַתָּ וּבָנִיתָ מָצוֹר עַל־הָעִיר אֲשֶׁר־הִוא עֹשָׂה עִמְּךָ מִלְחָמָה עַד רִדְתָּהּ:

19. When in your war against a city you have to besiege it a long time in order to capture it, you must not destroy its trees, wielding the ax against them. You may eat of them, but you must not cut them down. Are trees of the field human to withdraw before you into the besieged city?

20. Only trees that you know do not yield food may be destroyed; you may cut them down for constructing siegeworks against the city that is waging war on you, until it has been reduced.

Maimonides, *Mishneh Torah* "Laws of Kings and Their Wars" 6:8

אֵין קוֹצְצִין אִילָנֵי מַאֲכָל שֶׁחוּץ לַמְּדִינָה וְאֵין מוֹנְעִין מֵהֶם אַמַּת הַמַּיִם כְּדֵי שֶׁיִּיבְשׁוּ, שֶׁנֶּאֱמַר: לֹא תַשְׁחִית אֶת עֵצָהּ; וְכָל הַקּוֹצֵץ—לוֹקֶה. וְלֹא בְמָצוֹר בִּלְבָד,

אֶלָּא בְּכָל מָקוֹם כָּל הַקוֹצֵץ אִילָן מַאֲכָל דֶּרֶךְ הַשְׁחָתָה – לוֹקֶה; אֲבָל קוֹצְצִין אוֹתוֹ אִם הָיָה מַזִּיק אִילָנוֹת אֲחֵרִים, אוֹ מִפְּנֵי שֶׁמַּזִּיק בִּשְׂדֵה אֲחֵרִים, אוֹ מִפְּנֵי שֶׁדָּמָיו יְקָרִים. לֹא אָסְרָה תוֹרָה אֶלָּא דֶּרֶךְ הַשְׁחָתָה.

It is forbidden to cut down fruit-bearing trees outside a (besieged) city, nor may a water channel be deflected from them so they wither, as it is said: "You shall not destroy its trees" (Deuteronomy 20:19). Whoever cuts down a fruit-bearing tree is flogged. This penalty is imposed not only for cutting it down during a siege; whenever a fruit-yielding tree is cut down with destructive intent, flogging is incurred. It may be cut down, however, if it causes damage to other trees or to a field belonging to another person or if its value for other purposes is greater (than the fruit it produces). The law forbids only wanton destruction.

Maimonides, *Mishneh Torah*
"Laws of Kings and Their Wars" 6:10

וְלֹא הָאִילָנוֹת בִּלְבָד, אֶלָּא כָּל הַמְשַׁבֵּר כֵּלִים וְקוֹרֵעַ בְּגָדִים וְהוֹרֵס בִּנְיָן וְסוֹתֵם מַעְיָן וּמְאַבֵּד מַאֲכָלוֹת דֶּרֶךְ

הַשְׁחָתָה—עוֹבֵר בְּלֹא תַשְׁחִית, וְאֵינוֹ לוֹקֶה אֶלָּא
מַכַּת־מַרְדוּת מִדִּבְרֵיהֶם.

Not only one who cuts down (fruit-producing) trees, but
also one who smashes household goods, tears clothes,
demolishes a building, stops up a spring, or destroys
articles of food with destructive intent, transgresses the
command "You shall not destroy." He is not flogged,
but is administered a disciplinary beating imposed by
the Rabbis.

Questions and Commentary

Questions

1. What distinction between trees does the Bible make? What is the reason given to explain why trees should be spared?

2. In the eyes of Maimonides, what is the basic sin one commits when cutting down a fruit-bearing tree?

3. What might be mitigating circumstances that would allow the removal of such trees?

4. Maimonides writes that other destruction is also forbidden. Why is there a difference in the severity of the punishment meted out by the Sages?

Commentary

Destruction of the enemy's fruit trees was common practice in ancient times. Destroying the trees weakened the economic health of the community and might increase psychological pressure on the besieged city. Such practice is forbidden in Deuteronomy 20:19–20 (i.e., the attacking army must not destroy the enemy's trees), and the destructive spirit is expanded in later Rabbinic literature to include other needless destruction. There also seems to be compassion for the trees themselves, as suggested by the biblical question, "Are trees of the field human...?"

The Bible recognizes that there can be legitimate uses of trees in a siege, such as when a blockade wall must be constructed.

However, it is not acceptable to use trees that bear fruit for such a wall. It seems strange for the Bible to say that certain trees should be spared because they are not human, while allowing other trees to be destroyed. The question of whether or not a tree can be destroyed thus seems to be tied to its usefulness to human beings. Fruit-bearing trees are too important to destroy, even if they might wind up feeding the enemy.

Maimonides takes this biblical admonition and extends it to refer to any useful item. This destruction presumably applies to peacetime as well as war. In the Rabbinic tradition, this ideal acquired a name: *bal tashchit*. *Bal tashchit* teaches us not to wantonly destroy anything useful, regardless of whether it is natural or made by humans.

What Do You Think?

General History

Napalm is a flammable, gas-based weapon that is slow burning, ensuring greater destruction. This material was used by the U.S. Army in Vietnam in order to wipe out the enemy by destroying the land in which the enemy was embedded. The use of napalm by the United States in Vietnam was very controversial. Do you think there is ever justification for such "slash and burn" tactics? In addition, how should nuclear aggression—or defense—be considered in light of the biblical teachings above?

Israeli History

Is Israel justified in building a fence that will partition itself from the West Bank, even though this entails marring the landscape, including cutting through orchards of fruit-bearing trees and fields of crops? What might the passage from Deuteronomy 20 teach in regard to the security fence? Is this contradicted by any other biblical passages studied in previous chapters?

Additional Texts

1. II Chronicles 32:1–4

אַחֲרֵי הַדְּבָרִים וְהָאֱמֶת הָאֵלֶּה בָּא סַנְחֵרִיב מֶלֶךְ־
אַשּׁוּר וַיָּבֹא בִיהוּדָה וַיִּחַן עַל־הֶעָרִים הַבְּצֻרוֹת וַיֹּאמֶר
לְבִקְעָם אֵלָיו: ²וַיַּרְא יְחִזְקִיָּהוּ כִּי־בָא סַנְחֵרִיב וּפָנָיו
לַמִּלְחָמָה עַל־יְרוּשָׁלָ͏ִם: ³וַיִּוָּעַץ עִם־שָׂרָיו וְגִבֹּרָיו
לִסְתּוֹם אֶת־מֵימֵי הָעֲיָנוֹת אֲשֶׁר מִחוּץ לָעִיר
וַיַּעְזְרוּהוּ: ⁴וַיִּקָּבְצוּ עַם־רָב וַיִּסְתְּמוּ אֶת־כָּל־הַמַּעְיָנוֹת
וְאֶת־הַנַּחַל הַשּׁוֹטֵף בְּתוֹךְ־הָאָרֶץ לֵאמֹר לָמָּה יָבוֹאוּ
מַלְכֵי אַשּׁוּר וּמָצְאוּ מַיִם רַבִּים:

91

1. After these things, and these deeds of integrity, Sennacherib king of Assyria came, and entered into Judah, and encamped against the fortified cities, and thought to win them for himself.

2. And when Hezekiah saw that Sennacherib had come, and that he intended to fight against Jerusalem,

3. he took counsel with his princes and his mighty men to plug the waters of the springs that were outside the city; and they helped him.

4. And many people gathered together, and plugged all the springs, and the brook that ran through the midst of the land, saying, "Why should the kings of Assyria come and find much water?"

2. II Chronicles 32:30

וְהוּא יְחִזְקִיָּהוּ סָתַם אֶת־מוֹצָא מֵימֵי גִיחוֹן הָעֶלְיוֹן
וַיַּישְׁרֵם לְמַטָּה־מַּעְרָבָה לְעִיר דָּוִיד

This same Hezekiah also plugged the upper watercourse of Gihon and brought it straight down to the west side of the City of David.

3. Babylonian Talmud, *P'sachim* 56a

תָּנוּ רַבָּנַן: שִׁשָּׁה דְּבָרִים עָשָׂה חִזְקִיָּה הַמֶּלֶךְ, עַל
שְׁלשָׁה הוֹדוּ לוֹ וְעַל שְׁלשָׁה לֹא הוֹדוּ לוֹ... סָתַם מֵי
גִיחוֹן הָעֶלְיוֹן — וְלֹא הוֹדוּ לוֹ.

Our Rabbis taught: Six things King Hezekiah did; in three they (the Sages) agreed with him, and in three they did not agree with him...and he closed the waters of Upper Gihon, and they did not agree with him.

4. Scientists swarmed into the city. Some of them measured the force that had been necessary to shift marble gravestones in the cemeteries, to knock over twenty-two of the forty-seven railroads cars in the yards at Hiroshima station, to lift and move the concrete roadway of pressure exerted by the explosion varied from 5.3 to 8.0 tons per square yard. Others found that mica, of which the melting point is 900 decrees C, had fused on granite gravestones three hundred and eighty yards from the center; that telephone poles...whose carbonization temperature is 240 degrees C, had been charred at forty-four hundred yards from the center; and that the surface of gray clay tiles of the type used in Hiroshima, whose melting point is 1,300 degrees C, had dissolved at six hundred yards; and, after examining other significant ashes and melted bits, they concluded that the bomb's heat on the ground at the center must have been 6,000 degrees C....They estimated that, even with the primitive bomb used at Hiroshima, it would require a shelter of concrete fifty inches thick to protect a human being entirely from radiation sickness.

John Hershey, "Hiroshima," in *The New Yorker Book of War Pieces* (New York: Schocken Books, 1947), p. 557

5. The category of *milhemet reshuth* includes wars against the avowed enemies of Israel, nations that flagrantly violate the Seven Commandments and recognize no international obligations. This kind of war may be declared only after the Sanhedrin of seventy-one, the highest tribunal in Israel, the king of Israel, and the high-priest through the Urim and Thummim have given their approval. Its purpose may not be conquest, plunder, or destruction. It may be waged only for the protection of Israel and for the sanctification of the name of God, that is, the imposition of the Seven Commandments... No war may be waged against a nation that has not attacked Israel, or that lives up to the fundamentals of the Universal Religion. Even Edom, Ammon, and Moab, who had throughout their history displayed hostility to Israel, were not to be attacked, not to speak of those nations who were not bellicose. It would seem that the *milhemeth reshuth* was limited by the ideal boundaries of the Holy Land.

David S. Shapiro, "The Jewish Attitude Towards War and Peace," in *Israel of Tomorrow*, ed. Leo Jung (New York: Herald Square Press, 1946), p. 237

Making Peace

Even a casual reading of the Bible reveals that Judaism does not embrace peace over all other values. There is a time for war. Nevertheless, from its early period through today, Jewish texts consistently have championed the value of peace. The great Hebrew prophets, the exhortations of the Talmud, and the daily prayers of the worship service speak of pursuing peace and praise God as the Creator of peace. As a value, peace is celebrated in Jewish tradition.

Shalom may be the most well-known Hebrew word. Such texts in Jewish tradition as the following reflect the essential love of peace embraced by Judaism:

> It shall come to pass in days to come . . . that they shall beat their swords into plowshares and their spears into pruning hooks. Nation shall not lift up sword against nation, neither shall they learn war any more. . . . There will be no harm or destruction in all My holy mountain; for the land shall be full of the knowledge of Adonai as the waters cover the sea.
>
> Isaiah 2:2, 2:4, 11:9

Great is peace, for all blessings are contained in it....
Great is peace...for God's name is peace....

Vayikra Rabbah 9:9

It is written, SEEK PEACE AND PURSUE IT (Psalm 34:15).
The Law does not command you to run after or
pursue the other commandments, but only to fulfill
them upon the appropriate occasion. But peace you
must seek in your own place and pursue it even to
another place as well.

B'midbar Rabbah 19:27

In real life, however, peace is not easy to attain. Peace must
compete with other important values, such as justice and
security. The Jewish ideal was that peace would be seriously
contemplated before engaging in war. Indeed, peace was
always the goal of the Talmudic Rabbis. Even in matters of
self-defense, the besieged nation was first supposed to work
toward peace. The following biblical text depicts Moses's
recollection of seeking peace before war.

Text

Deuteronomy 2:26–34

‏26וָאֶשְׁלַח מַלְאָכִים מִמִּדְבַּר קְדֵמוֹת אֶל־סִיחוֹן מֶלֶךְ‏
‏חֶשְׁבּוֹן דִּבְרֵי שָׁלוֹם לֵאמֹר: 27אֶעְבְּרָה בְאַרְצֶךָ בַּדֶּרֶךְ‏

בַּדֶּרֶךְ אֵלֵךְ לֹא אָסוּר יָמִין וּשְׂמֹאול: 28אֹכֶל בַּכֶּסֶף
תַּשְׁבִּרֵנִי וְאָכַלְתִּי וּמַיִם בַּכֶּסֶף תִּתֶּן־לִי וְשָׁתִיתִי רַק
אֶעְבְּרָה בְרַגְלָי: 29כַּאֲשֶׁר עָשׂוּ־לִי בְּנֵי עֵשָׂו הַיֹּשְׁבִים
בְּשֵׂעִיר וְהַמּוֹאָבִים הַיֹּשְׁבִים בְּעָר עַד אֲשֶׁר־אֶעֱבֹר אֶת־
הַיַּרְדֵּן אֶל־הָאָרֶץ אֲשֶׁר־יְהֹוָה אֱלֹהֵינוּ נֹתֵן לָנוּ: 30וְלֹא
אָבָה סִיחֹן מֶלֶךְ חֶשְׁבּוֹן הַעֲבִרֵנוּ בּוֹ כִּי־הִקְשָׁה יְהֹוָה
אֱלֹהֶיךָ אֶת־רוּחוֹ וְאִמֵּץ אֶת־לְבָבוֹ לְמַעַן תִּתּוֹ בְיָדְךָ
כַּיּוֹם הַזֶּה: 31וַיֹּאמֶר יְהֹוָה אֵלַי רְאֵה הַחִלֹּתִי תֵּת לְפָנֶיךָ
אֶת־סִיחֹן וְאֶת־אַרְצוֹ הָחֵל רָשׁ לָרֶשֶׁת אֶת־אַרְצוֹ:
32וַיֵּצֵא סִיחֹן לִקְרָאתֵנוּ הוּא וְכָל־עַמּוֹ לַמִּלְחָמָה
יָהְצָה: 33וַיִּתְּנֵהוּ יְהֹוָה אֱלֹהֵינוּ לְפָנֵינוּ וַנַּךְ אֹתוֹ וְאֶת־
בָּנָו [בָּנָיו] וְאֶת־כָּל־עַמּוֹ: 34וַנִּלְכֹּד אֶת־כָּל־עָרָיו בָּעֵת
הַהִוא וַנַּחֲרֵם אֶת־כָּל־עִיר מְתִם וְהַנָּשִׁים וְהַטָּף לֹא
הִשְׁאַרְנוּ שָׂרִיד:

26. Then I sent messengers from the wilderness of Kedemoth to King Sihon of Heshbon with an offer of peace, as follows,

27. "Let me pass through your country. I will keep strictly to the highway, turning off neither to the right nor to the left.

28. What food I eat you will supply for money, and

what water I drink you will furnish for money; just let me pass through—

29. as the descendants of Esau who dwell in Seir did for me, and the Moabites who dwell in Ar—that I may cross the Jordan into the land that the Eternal our God is giving us."

30. But King Sihon of Heshbon refused to let us pass through, because the Eternal had stiffened his will and hardened his heart in order to deliver him into your power—as is now the case.

31. And the Eternal One said to me: See, I begin by placing Sihon and his land at your disposal. Begin the occupation; take possession of his land.

32. Sihon with all his troops took the field against us at Jahaz,

33. and the Eternal our God delivered him to us and we defeated him and his sons and all his troops.

34. At that time we captured all his towns, and we doomed every town—men, women, and children—leaving no survivor.

Moses, remembering an earlier campaign, recalls that he requested safe passage for the Israelites through the land ruled by King Sihon. He even agrees to pay for food and water. Nevertheless, the king wants to fight, and so Moses and the Israelites defeat them. Moses's decision to first attempt a peaceful resolution is the subject of the following midrashic comment.

D'varim Rabbah 5:12 (Margoliot Edition)

הַקָּדוֹשׁ־בָּרוּךְ־הוּא אָמַר לוֹ שֶׁיִּלָּחֵם עִם סִיחוֹן וְעוֹג,
שֶׁנֶּאֱמַר "וְהִתְגָּר בּוֹ מִלְחָמָה", הוּא לֹא עָשָׂה כֵן, אֶלָּא
"וָאֶשְׁלַח מַלְאָכִים מִמִּדְבַּר קְדֵמוֹת אֶל סִיחוֹן מֶלֶךְ
חֶשְׁבּוֹן דִּבְרֵי שָׁלוֹם לֵאמֹר", אָמַר לוֹ הַקָּדוֹשׁ־בָּרוּךְ־
הוּא: אָמַרְתִּי לְךָ לְהִלָּחֵם עִמּוֹ וְאַתָּה פָּתַחְתָּ לוֹ
בְּשָׁלוֹם, חַיֶּיךָ שֶׁאֲנִי מְקַיֵּם גְּזֵרָתֶךָ: כָּל מִלְחָמָה שֶׁיִּהְיוּ
הוֹלְכִין לֹא יְהוּ פּוֹתְחִין אֶלָּא בְּשָׁלוֹם, שֶׁנֶּאֱמַר "כִּי
תִקְרַב אֶל עִיר" וְגוֹ'.

God told Moses to fight against Sihon and Og, as it is
written: ENGAGE THEM IN WAR. But he did not do so.
Rather he sent emissaries of peace to Sihon, the king of
Heshbon. The Holy One of Blessing declared: I told you
to fight them, but you tried to make peace. By your life,
I make a decree that each war shall first be preceded by
attempts at peace, as it is written: When you approach a
city (to make war)....

Questions and Commentary

Questions

1. What is the behavior of Moses that the midrash addresses?

2. How does God respond to Moses's behavior, according to the midrash?

3. What lesson concerning peace does the midrash wish to teach?

Commentary

The midrash reflects the Rabbinical desire to temper the severity of war in the Bible with a more humane approach to enemies both potential and real. Therefore it applauds Moses's decision to first attempt a peaceful resolution—even if this contradicted the word of God! Moreover, the midrash imagines that God is pleased with the decision and learns from Moses to order the Israelites to always seek a peaceful solution first, except in the case of the seven nations and the Amalekites. It should be noted that in the Bible, peaceful resolution usually meant the enemy city would surrender. It was not a peace between equals, but it did avoid violence. Presumably, later Rabbinic tradition preferred to imagine peaceful cohabitation, not surrender of the other through threat of force.

What Do You Think?

General History

In 1938 England attempted to address Hitler's aggression with the Munich Agreement, condemned by many at the time and proved by history to be disastrous. The agreement allowed Hitler to "peacefully" capture Czechoslovakia. In the fall of 1938, the prime minister of England, Neville Chamberlain, declared "peace in our time" as a result of the agreement. The Nazis, of course, were not content to stop their aggression there. What some see as peace others see as appeasement. Where do we draw the line?

Israeli History

How much is Israel expected to give up in order to make peace with her neighbors? Was the peace agreement with Egypt, the Camp David Accords, worthwhile? What about the agreement with Jordan? What about the terms offered, though not accepted, by the Palestinians? Does the withdrawal of Israel from the Gaza Strip reflect a policy of appeasement?

Additional Texts

1. Isaiah 2:2–4

²וְהָיָ֣ה ׀ בְּאַחֲרִ֣ית הַיָּמִ֗ים נָכ֨וֹן יִֽהְיֶ֜ה הַ֤ר בֵּית־יְהוָה֙ בְּרֹ֣אשׁ הֶהָרִ֔ים וְנִשָּׂ֖א מִגְּבָע֑וֹת וְנָהֲר֥וּ אֵלָ֖יו כָּל־הַגּוֹיִֽם׃ ³וְֽהָלְכ֞וּ עַמִּ֣ים רַבִּ֗ים וְאָמְרוּ֙ לְכ֣וּ ׀ וְנַעֲלֶ֣ה אֶל־הַר־יְהוָ֗ה אֶל־בֵּית֙ אֱלֹהֵ֣י יַעֲקֹ֔ב וְיֹרֵ֙נוּ֙ מִדְּרָכָ֔יו וְנֵלְכָ֖ה בְּאֹרְחֹתָ֑יו כִּ֤י מִצִּיּוֹן֙ תֵּצֵ֣א תוֹרָ֔ה וּדְבַר־יְהוָ֖ה מִירוּשָׁלָֽ͏ִם׃ ⁴וְשָׁפַט֙ בֵּ֣ין הַגּוֹיִ֔ם וְהוֹכִ֖יחַ לְעַמִּ֣ים רַבִּ֑ים וְכִתְּת֨וּ חַרְבוֹתָ֜ם לְאִתִּ֗ים וַחֲנִיתֽוֹתֵיהֶם֙ לְמַזְמֵר֔וֹת לֹא־יִשָּׂ֨א ג֤וֹי אֶל־גּוֹי֙ חֶ֔רֶב וְלֹא־יִלְמְד֥וּ ע֖וֹד מִלְחָמָֽה׃

2. And it shall come to pass in the last days, that the mountain of the Eternal's House shall be established on the top of the mountains and shall be exalted above the hills; and all nations shall flow to it.

3. And many people shall go and say, "Come, and let us go up to the mountain of the Eternal One, to the House of the God of Jacob; and God will teach us the Eternal's ways, and we will walk in God's paths; for from Zion shall go forth Torah, and the word of the Eternal One from Jerusalem.

4. And God shall judge among the nations and shall decide for many people; and they shall beat their swords into plowshares, and their spears into pruning hooks; nation shall not lift up sword against nation, nor shall they learn war any more.

2. Let me say to you, the Palestinians, we are destined to live together on the same soil in the same land. We, the soldiers who have returned from battles stained with blood; we who have seen our relatives and friends killed before our eyes; we who have attended their funerals and cannot look into the eyes of their parents; we who have come from a land where parents bury their children; we who have fought against you, the Palestinians, we, say to you today in a loud and clear voice, enough of blood and tears. Enough!

> Israeli Prime Minister Yitzchak Rabin, the White House, September 1993, after signing a peace treaty with the Palestinian Authority

3. Peace is first of all in our prayers, but it is also the aspiration of the Jewish people, a genuine aspiration for peace.

There are enemies of peace who are trying to hurt us, in order to torpedo the peace process.

I want to say bluntly, that we have found a partner for peace among the Palestinians as well: the PLO, which was an enemy, and has ceased to engage in terrorism. Without partners for peace, there can be no peace.

We will demand that they do their part for peace, just as we will do our part for peace, in order to solve the most complicated, prolonged, and emotionally charged aspect of the Israeli-Arab conflict: the Palestinian-Israeli conflict.

This is a course which is fraught with difficulties and pain. For Israel, there is no path that is without pain.

But the path of peace is preferable to the path of war.

I say this to you as one who was a military man, someone who is today Minister of Defense and sees the pain of the families of the IDF soldiers. For them, for our children, in my case for our grandchildren, I want this government to exhaust every opening, every possibility, to promote and achieve a comprehensive peace. Even with Syria, it will be possible to make peace.

This rally must send a message to the Israeli people, to the Jewish people around the world, to the many people in the Arab world, and indeed to the entire world, that the Israeli people want peace, support peace.

Final Speech of Yitzchak Rabin, November 4, 1995,
Tel Aviv City Hall Plaza; cited in Hagshama,
Department of the World Zionist Organization,
www.hagshama.org.il/en/resources/view.asp?id=171

Conclusion

The texts in this book, by no means exhaustive, are intended to provide an introduction into the views of war and peace as they developed in Jewish history. What did we learn? Certainly it is clear that these views developed over time, but the general trends are found as early as the Bible. There are three types of war: obligatory wars (divinely ordained by God and referring to the seven Canaanite nations and the Amalekites); optional wars (started by the king in order to obtain more land and authorized by the Sanhedrin, the High Priest, and the *Urim* and *Tumim*); and commanded wars (for self-defense). A fourth, related category involves preemptive war, which in effect straddles the boundary between optional and self-defensive wars.

Jewish heritage, as it unfolded, understood that only a war of self-defense was possible after the fall of the Second Temple. The authors of the Talmud, midrash, and later texts were not soldiers themselves. They were scholars, and therefore it is not surprising that they envisioned a world of peace as the ideal. Indeed, not living in a world with Jewish power, it was easier for them to concentrate on the values of peace.

In conclusion, consider the following text from the Bible and its midrashic interpretation. One of the oldest parts of the Bible is the Song of the Sea, describing the rescue of the Israelites from Egyptian bondage. This poem celebrates God's active role in destroying the Egyptians.

זְיְהוָֹה אִישׁ מִלְחָמָה יְהוָֹה שְׁמוֹ: ⁴מַרְכְּבֹת פַּרְעֹה וְחֵילוֹ
יָרָה בַיָּם וּמִבְחַר שָׁלִשָׁיו טֻבְּעוּ בְיַם־סוּף:

3. The Eternal, the Warrior—Eternal One is His Name!
4. Pharaoh's chariots and his army He has cast into the sea; and the pick of his officers are drowned in the Sea of Reeds.

Exodus 15:3–4

In response to this obvious approval for the suffering of the Egyptians, the Babylonian Talmud imagines the following dialogue occurring in heaven:

בְּאוֹתָהּ שָׁעָה בִּקְשׁוּ מַלְאֲכֵי הַשָּׁרֵת לוֹמַר שִׁירָה לִפְנֵי
הַקָּדוֹשׁ בָּרוּךְ הוּא, אָמַר לָהֶן הַקָּדוֹשׁ בָּרוּךְ הוּא:
מַעֲשֵׂה יָדַי טוֹבְעִין בַּיָּם וְאַתֶּם אוֹמְרִים שִׁירָה לְפָנַי?!

In the instant [that God drowned the Egyptians] the ministering angels wished to utter song before the Holy One, but He rebuked them, saying, "The works of My hands are drowning in the sea, and you would utter song in My presence!"

Babylonian Talmud, *Sanhedrin* 39b

Nothing better reflects the transition in Jewish thought from God's celebration of war to God's regret of violence than this imagined rebuke. In effect, God is saying to the angels (and to us): I know there have been times when aggressive war was required, but such times no longer exist—nor will they ever return. The only type of war that is acceptable is one of self defense. But this, too, is a great pity. Would that all could sit at home, enjoying their house, their vineyard, their spouse and family, sitting under their fig tree, with none to make them afraid.

Glossary of Terms and Sources

aggadah Narrative portions of Rabbinic literature. These can be stories that expand the biblical narrative or that describe the actions and beliefs of the ancient Rabbis.

Babylonian Talmud A compilation of Rabbinic teachings dealing with law, ethics, rituals, holidays, biblical interpretation, and many other subjects. Compiled around the year 500 C.E.

halachah Jewish law. Such laws are found in the Bible and in Rabbinic literature such as the Mishnah, Talmud, and medieval legal codes.

Chizkiya ben Manoach Also known as Chizkuni, a twelfth-century Jewish scholar who lived in France.

Isaac ben Moses Viennese Jewish legal scholar (1180–1250) and author of *Sefer Or Zarua*, an important halachic work.

Kohein Gadol High Priest, and as such the head of the Temple sacrificial cult in Jerusalem.

Maimonides Also known as Rambam, Rabbi Moses ben Maimon (1135–1204) lived in Egypt. His numerous works include his *Mishneh Torah*, a complete summary of Jewish law.

Menachem HaMeiri Provencal scholar and commentator on the Talmud (1249–1306). His works included halachic rulings, Talmudic exposition, and biblical interpretation.

midrash Interpretation of a biblical text. *Midrash halachah* offers exposition of legal sections of the Bible, such as the laws of the Sabbath. An example is *Sifra*, a commentary on the legal portions of Leviticus. *Midrash aggadah* centers on nonlegal biblical material and is used for nonlegal purposes. An example of a midrashic work is *Midrash Rabbah* to Genesis. (See also **aggadah**.)

milchamah Hebrew for "war."

milchemet chovah An obligatory war. The term applies to the Israelite war of conquest against the seven Canaanite nations and Amalek.

milchemet mitzvah Lit., a "commanded war," applied to wars of defense.

milchemet reshut Lit., an "authorized war" or an "optional war," concerning expansionary wars such as the ones fought by King David.

Mishnah Consolidation of Rabbinic law, edited by Rabbi Judah HaNasi, ca. 200 C.E. The Mishnah constitutes the first part, or core, of the Talmud.

m'shuach milchamah   The *kohein* (priest) appointed to speak to the troops before battle.

Nachmanides   Also known as Ramban, Rabbi Moses ben Nachman (1194–1270) lived in Spain. His various works include a commentary on the Torah.

pikuach nefesh   Saving a life. This principle, found in the Babylonian Talmud, *Yoma* 84b, overrides the laws of Shabbat.

responsum (pl., responsa)   Answers of a rabbinic authority to questions relating to Jewish law.

Sanhedrin   Court of seventy-one sages in ancient Judea.

seven nations   The seven Canaanite nations ordered to be destroyed.

shalom   Hebrew for "peace," from the root *sh-l-m*, conveying healing (i.e., being complete or whole).

Sifra, Sifrei D'varim   Early Rabbinic interpretations of biblical law, for the books of Leviticus and Deuteronomy, respectively. These collections of *midrash halachah* were compiled in Palestine in approximately the third century C.E.

Urim and Tumim   The breastplate of the High Priest, considered to have the power of an oracle. See Numbers 27:21.